LOSING A SPOUSE
A WIDOWER'S WAY

Dennis Disselkoen

Dennis Disselkoen

Losing a Spouse

A Widower's Way

Help in coping during her last days and in the days ahead

For My Children

Wesley David
Michele Renee
Joel Nathan

Dennis Disselkoen

Table of Contents

PREFACE

Purpose and Process

This book was written for every man who has or soon will share my experience of losing his wife, and also for his friends and family members who wish to support those men in their challenging adjustment. Men who lose their wives to a fatal accident or a rapidly deteriorating medical condition face an avalanche of emotion in a relatively short time –a few weeks or a few days. Other men whose wives endure the slow progression of terminal illness must experience an extended period of anticipatory grief as well as the grief following the loss of their wives. And finally, the friends and family members who comprise a man's support system may not know what to say and may struggle with the question of what assistance is appropriate. It will be my goal to bring understanding and practical suggestions to all three groups on the pages that follow.

This effort is a result of my reflecting on my experience over a number of years in caring for my late wife; of interacting with medical professionals, concerned church members, well-meaning friends, immediate family, curious neighbors and distant relatives. I did not take notes or keep a journal during the time of my wife's decline with the view of writing a book about my experiences. That was never in view, but as I had hours to reflect on what had happened – and in some respects is still happening – I wanted to write my thoughts as a kind of personal therapy. Frankly, I expected to deal with my loss a lot better than I did. After the death of my wife I was exhausted mentally and emotionally. Accepting my change in marital status was a matter for my mind. I had become a widower. My wife and I had been married for nearly forty-seven years, so I found it hard to think of myself as not married. The emotional side of things surprised me. I was lonely for a very long while prior to the death of my wife; I was sad most of the time though I masked it. I was faced with staggering change in the days, months and years ahead.

My wife and I had come to share life's joys and sorrows; we had come to agree on an economy of living, helping each other in the responsibilities of living; both of us "specializing" in particular tasks. I expect that such is the case with most couples who have been married for any length of time. As a widower, I would have to assume the roles and responsibilities my wife had taken on. I realize that there are thousands upon thousands of men in precisely the same situation as I. To be sure, some are coping with loss better than I and some are not doing as well in adjusting to life without a wife. Various factors account for the differences; I cannot begin to address them all. Some still have children under the roof; others face "the four walls" by themselves. I thought that perhaps, if I could write a brief but helpful book for the benefit of those who grieve and for those around them, it would be a worthy service.

There is also a need for a resource like this. As of this writing, data available shows that there are 13.7 million widowed persons in the United States. Over 11 million of these are women. Presently, the ratio of widows to widowers is four to one.[1] There are several reasons for this: first, "... because their death rate is lower than men's, larger numbers of women survive into advanced years. Second, wives are generally younger than their husbands, a fact that increases their probability of surviving their spouses even without the differences in longevity. Third, among the widowed, remarriage rates are significantly lower for women than [they are for] men. Therefore, many men leave widower status by wedding again, whereas many women do not, thereby adding to the surplus of female survivors."[2]

Though there are roughly 2.75 million widowers in the United States alone, widowers are a neglected group. Characteristically, they do not have circles of friends with whom they discuss the emotional side of things. To understate, men often keep conversation on the light side of things; shallow-speak is the order of the day. Men's tendency to be private with their feelings can have two unfortunate outcomes: it deprives them of potential sources of support, and in so doing also makes it difficult for their would-be allies to help to ease their pain. *Generally* speaking they tend less to seek help, advice, or direction from others. There are exceptions of course. By and large, however, men find themselves isolated. Perhaps it is the "I-can-handle-it" mentality, or the macho mentality that makes it so difficult for men in the time of grief to turn to others for help. Even though at times men realize that there could be a benefit in seeking assistance from others, they keep to themselves and often withdraw. Certainly, for some, the thought of seeking help simply does not occur to them.

Women, on the other hand, *seem* more gregarious. They seem more open to sharing their hearts and heartaches with friends, whether deliberately setting up networks for help or not. Women seem to bare and share, to have close friends with whom they can bare their souls, with whom they share their troubles. They go to their friends to "unload". Their friends commiserate, comfort, and counsel them. When their marriages end in the death of their husbands, a cadre of close friends has already been in place. Men "go it alone" often to their own detriment. Perhaps a man's facility at keeping a stiff upper lip allows other men and women to participate in the deception that all is well.

What's more, both men and women seem more hesitant to approach a man who has recently become widowed in order to offer help than they are to make the same offer to women who have become widows. And, even when approach does occur, help is little more than words of sympathy. Guys tend not to approach guys about these things and it is no surprise that women feel reluctant to inquire too deeply about a widower's troubled heart.

Credits, thanks, acknowledgements, appreciations

I wish to thank the men who volunteered to be interviewed, whose insights and cooperation were invaluable; to Lori McMillen who continues a vital ministry to the grieving at the Christ Community Church in Hudson, Ohio. Her insights were beneficial as I initiated the work; to Anna S. Canada who was a sounding board and offered encouragement to me in the early stages of the effort; to Phyllis Howat who helped me in reading and suggesting changes to the manuscript; to my many friends who indirectly aided me with an occasional prodding question: "How's the book coming along?"; and, to the publisher, and especially to Dr. Kriss Wiant whose literary sense and professional acumen were of immeasurable value. His help did more to sharpen my writing focus than I expected. I am profoundly grateful for his counsel. Without the help of these and others, this book would not have become a reality.

INTRODUCTION

The core of the material for the booklet comes from my own experience, but I did want to be able to offer a wider expression of what a man goes through when he loses his wife. No two men experience that lost in exactly the same way; no grieving is identical to another's grieving. However, there is sufficient commonness in losing a wife to be able to recognize similarities and to draw some conclusions. To gain a sampling of that commonness, I interviewed ten men who had lost their wives. The length of time individual interviewees had been widowers ranged from one year to fourteen years. Ages of the interviewees ranged from fifty-four to eighty-two. I developed a protocol of thirty-five questions, which was used as a basis for interviewing. Interview sessions were recorded and transcribed by me. These questions are included in Appendix A. Names of participants in the interview process and names of their late wives were assigned aliases to protect their identities. Permission to use comments from interview sessions was granted by each interviewee. When I quote from a response to one of the protocol questions, the initials of the aliases are used to identify the respondent. Needless to say, some men were rather brief in their answers whereas others were more verbose. I am grateful for the willingness of those men to talk with me about the past and ongoing experiences of their sorrows and joys; to share the time of perhaps the greatest grief they had experienced in their lives. Their contributions enriched this book.

The names of physicians, hospitals and healthcare facilities, states and towns were omitted further to protect the identity of the interviewees and their families.

I also read literature on grief, mourning, living with loss, living alone after loving, etc., the titles of which appear at the close of this work. I hope this brief effort will benefit both those who are grieving the loss of their wives, and those about to enter into that grief. It may also be a helpful resource in the hands of those who want to console their grieving friends. The suggestions I present are not exclusively mine, but emerged from comments of the interviewees as well as from the various writings cited, and special professional consult.

I have attempted to cover some of the struggles men face as they find themselves alone. The loss of a wife bears on a man physically, spiritually, socially and emotionally. This book is not primarily a book on grief and coping with loss; bookstore shelves are full of them. Certainly, grief is the experience of all who have lost loved ones, and though I address this aspect of loss, I did not want my observations and suggestions to be the book's primary focus.

As far as the structure of the book is concerned, I have divided it into three parts: **Before** – the experience leading to the point of my wife's death; **During** – the experience at the time of my wife's death including arranging the funeral and the time shortly thereafter; and **After** – the time of adjustment and recovering after her death.

I have used brackets [] in three different ways: to indicate a word or a number of words that an interviewee did not speak but implied; to indicate the name of a city, state, institution, or medical professionals, the identities of which would impinge upon their privacy, or which if known would suggest a possible identity of an interviewee; to clarify what may otherwise not be clear about the remarks or the intentions of an interviewee. Unless otherwise indicated, all quotations from the Bible are from the English Standard Version.

BEFORE

Chapter One

How This Started

You do not know what tomorrow will bring. (James 4:14)

I met Grace at college. We were both involved in a campus ministry and over the weeks and months of activity together, we developed a mutual attraction. I asked her to go out for coffee. She said she didn't drink coffee, but would enjoy a cup of tea. That date was the first of many. I met her in September, asked her to marry me the following April and we were married in August of that same year. After I graduated, we struggled together through my seminary studies. She became a pastor's wife. The Lord blessed us with three children – two sons and a daughter. We have seven grandchildren. We were married nearly forty-seven years.

Grace didn't get sick very often. Both she and I enjoyed the blessing of good health. At a routine health check however, her blood pressure reading was extremely high. This alarmed the doctor who took a second reading. He asked about high blood pressure in the past and about her family history – had either of her parents had high blood pressure and, "Yes" both had. Perhaps there was a hereditary component to my wife's high blood pressure. The doctor prescribed medication and scheduled another appointment within a few weeks to monitor her.

When time for that follow-up came, her blood pressure had actually risen in spite of her having taken medicine to reduce it. An abdominal examination indicated the presence of a large mass and the need for a scan to determine what was actually present. The scan showed that a grapefruit-size mass had developed around the primary artery to her left kidney. It had basically cut off that kidney's blood supply and had caused Grace's blood pressure to spike. Eventually, Grace would lose the use of that kidney. The doctor said, "It looks as though you have a large mass that we'll need to address very soon." He scheduled and performed a needle biopsy and determined that the growth was cancerous.

He recommended that a bone marrow sample be taken to discover, if possible, exactly what kind of cancer was present.

We were numbed by the news of that diagnosis – non-Hodgkin's lymphoma. I cannot speak about what went through my wife's mind, but my imagination roamed freely for a few moments.

There was no weeping or wringing of hands. Instead, we were silent and realized that this diagnosis was the providence God had for us. One might say that we were in shock. Perhaps we were, but we also had a hardy confidence that God would direct us and help us through anything that he brought into our lives. I don't remember who broke the silence after we left the doctor's office. Most likely, I made a comment about seeing what the Lord would do. Frankly, it took a few days for the reality to sink in. We called our children and conveyed the news. They were filled with questions, most of which we could not answer. We asked them for their prayers. They assured us they would pray.

Since we were part of a community of faith, we wanted to let others know as well. The time for doing that came after a Sunday morning worship and Sunday school hour. I simply summarized the findings of the tests Grace had undergone and told the congregation what the doctors had said about the treatment. I asked for their prayers for us – that we wouldn't sin against God in anything we would say or do during the time of his testing and that God would receive glory. Our friends at the church assured us that they would be praying for us.

Many of our friends outside our immediate church family are praying Christians and would have wanted the opportunity to pray for us. We wanted to keep them informed as well, so I sent periodic emails to an extensive distribution list. This is the content of the first letter.

During a routine physical examination last week, Grace's doctor discovered a huge mass in her lower abdomen and ordered a couple of ultrasounds. Grace underwent those procedures and the radiologists suggested she have a CT scan as well. The scan showed a tumor about the size of cantaloupe. On Tuesday May 29, Grace had a biopsy done on that mass.

On Thursday Grace and I went to the oncologist to learn what the biopsy indicated. As we suspected, she does have lymphatic cancer. The tumor causes her stomach to protrude and gives her pain in her kidney. We also learned that it surrounds the aorta in her lower back.

The growth rate for the kind of lymphoma Grace has is intermediate. The doctor stated that he would initially treat the mass with a combination of three drugs plus a steroid. For some reason that combination of drugs and steroid is referred to as "CHOP"[1]. The doctor encouraged us that we could possibly see some reduction of the mass size within days or a couple of weeks.

As soon as Tuesday June 5th Grace will undergo her first round of chemo. We also were told that one of her kidneys is not operational, and that if the mass is reduced in size she may regain the use of her left kidney.

There will be hair loss after the second chemo treatment and it will last until the conclusion of the treatment cycle, which at this point looks like mid-September. So, Grace will be sporting a "Curly Howard" hairdo for the summer. The chemo will weaken her immune system significantly.

We ask for your prayers that the approach to treatment would be successful, and that Grace would be able to sustain the effects of the chemotherapy. Pray that God would give peace to Grace and to me throughout the entire experience.

My wife was scheduled for a bone marrow extraction, the procedure for which at the time was very painful. Lab results from that extraction showed that the cancer was a particular kind of non-Hodgkin's lymphoma and treatment was prescribed. We were told that the kind of cancer that she had was slow-growing but highly resistant to medical treatment. There would be a weekly treatment of CHOP for six weeks; then there would be several weeks where there would be no treatment at all, and then another six weeks of treatment and so on until another assessment could be made. Of course, the reason for the break in treatment is because the drugs greatly weaken a patient, and also compromise the immune system. The break in treatments allows a patient to recover sufficiently to undergo another round of treatment. During that time as well, medication is given to replace what was depleted in the blood; both white cells and red cells required a boost. My wife's immune system was compromised to the extent that she could receive no visitors and was discouraged from venturing out of the house very frequently. She could easily contract something that her body would not be able to fight off. Both of us understood that this intrusion would affect our lives, our futures together. During the treatment, my wife's energy level dropped dramatically. She developed sores on her gums and on the sides of her mouth. She did not want to eat because of the sores, and not eating regularly further weakened her.

I still remember the shriek I heard when she went to brush her hair and her hair came out. This was after the initial chemo treatments, after her first round of therapy. It was a shriek of dismay. In the days that followed, she lost all of her hair. She wore a bandana to cover up her hair loss. Later, a friend went with her to buy a wig, a wig she would wear until her own hair came back.

After about six months of treatment, there was another assessment. The tumor had been reduced significantly, but damage had already been done to her left kidney. A maintenance regimen was established so that Grace would not have to keep up a schedule of regular treatments. All seemed to be under control. The cancer seemed to be arrested and the doctors were going to "watch" her. Slowly she regained her energy and life continued as normal as can be expected when one has to deal with the reality of cancer.

We wanted to keep our larger circle of friends in the loop so I sent updated information and asked for continued prayer:

Grace did undergo her first Chemo treatment on the fifth of June, after which she became very ill for about a week. The bone marrow biopsy she had earlier in the day on the fifth indicated that indeed the cancer has gotten into her bone marrow; five percent of the marrow is cancerous. As of the moment, the doctor does not want to alter the composition of the chemo cocktail. What else became clear is that rather than the cancer being of intermediate growth, the additional lab samples show that the cancer is the slow growing variety. That means that Grace has had it longer than we expected. She undergoes another treatment on Tuesday, the twenty-sixth. Thank you for your cards, calls, and most of all, for your prayers. Please continue to pray!

After the third treatment, I sent another note to our praying friends:

I wanted to keep you posted about Grace's progress. Tuesday the seventeenth, she had her third chemo treatment … Results were back from her second CT scan, taken last Wednesday and the pictures show that the tumor has shrunk to about the size of an orange. Technically, this means that Grace has experienced "partial remission". We had hoped that she would regain use of her left kidney, but apparently she has lost use of that organ. Grace is in a good spirit most of the time. Keep us in your prayers.

An additional letter followed:

So many of you have called or written to enquire about Grace's health. Thank you for your on-going concern and prayers … Grace did experience a short hospitalization about a month ago, when her temperature rose to an unsafe height. Doctors medicated her and watched her for a couple of days, then sent her home. Her white blood cells have a way of disappearing; the low count at the last go around was 0.5. She is giving herself injections of Neupogen – a drug that enhances white cell production – in order to boost her immune system. She is also receiving a weekly injection of Procrit for boosting her red blood cells … Treatments really take a toll on Grace's energy level. For the most part her spirit is good. Keep her in your prayers.

We asked the obvious question: "What is the life expectancy?" The doctor(s) were understandably reluctant to give an answer; everyone's situation is different and, of course no physician wants either to be unduly optimistic or pessimistic, but the short answer was that about *seven* years was the best we could hope for. That was in 2001. In the providence of God, new drugs in the pipeline would become available to treat the three recurrences of the cancer over the following *fourteen* years. It seemed as though each time the cancer "came back," a new experimental drug had been approved for limited use. The return of the cancer each time was after about four and a half years of remission.

At the time of the initial diagnosis, my wife felt fine. There was no obvious pain or discomfort, but the reality of knowing she had what would be terminal cancer weighed heavily on both of us. Over the weeks and months and *years*, we visited the doctors together. We scheduled tests and treatments and I accompanied her as she underwent them.[2] We scheduled the taking of medications and she took them. In the early years of treatment – between those times of recurrence and when Grace's immune system indicated strength – we were able to travel. Activities resumed; shopping, socializing, house-holding and church involvement continued. The cancer growth had been and continued to be slow, but the growth did not stop. Medicines and treatments seemed merely to retard that growth for a time. Life went on as normal.

Offers of Help

If your wife has cancer or any other life-threatening condition and if you belong to a caring community of faith, you will receive numerous offers to help – to cook, to clean, to shop or to do errands. These offers to assist are expressions of care and concern. Your friends will ask what they can do and sometimes the only answer is "pray for God's mercy, pray for our faith to be strong during this time of testing, pray for the pain to subside, pray for strength and wisdom and peace". Your dear friends will want to bring meals, but near the end, your wife may not be able to eat the meals and you may notice that your own appetite for food has diminished as well.

Chapter Two

A New Normal

My grace is sufficient for you. (1Corinthians 12:9)

Unless the loss of your wife is unexpected and sudden there is time prior to her actual departure to face the inevitable together. The realization comes first to one and then to the other that your wife – your love, friend and confidant – will not get better. That realization may come after a prolonged illness or after numerous attempts through various means to effect a cure if your wife is battling some disease or physical malady. It is a sad and sobering time, a time when one or both of you may not want to talk about your feelings. The subject of one going and the other staying does not lend itself easily to speaking. So, there may be periods of awkward silence about this issue. Eventually however, the subject will surface and perhaps one of you will want to talk about it, but because the subject is just too painful, too depressing, too heavy, the other may not be ready or willing to talk about it. Nevertheless, together you will face what is known and certain.

The time came when Grace could not function in any meaningful way. She required help with everything. I was lonely for the person she was. It was so profoundly sad! I asked myself, "How can this be; how can I be lonely when she is just a few steps away from me?" I missed the kind of interaction I had had with her, I missed conversations, I missed looking forward with her to a future of retirement and relative freedom from a more fixed schedule.

Somehow, even in my wife's condition, the glory of God was involved. It may seem difficult to put those two ideas together, I know. What does the glory of God have to do with the inglorious misery of one of his creatures?

An incident in Jesus' ministry comes to my mind. It's the one about the man who was born blind. His condition was the object of a theological question of Jesus' disciples: "Rabbi, who, sinned, this man or his parents that he was born blind?"[1] – implying that those two were the only options to consider. The disciples' query reflected the current thought about the relationship of committing sin and experiencing particular afflictions as a result. The disciples believed that either the man's parents had sinned and were being punished by parenting a blind child for the rest of their lives – with all the added cares and concerns – or that the blind man himself had somehow sinned in his mother's womb and was "punished" with lifelong blindness.

Jesus explained that neither was the case. The man was born blind, "that the works of God might be displayed in him."[2] Certainly, if someone were to have explained this truth to the parents or later, to the man prior to the man's healing, they would have found it incredible until … until the man was healed of his blindness. The man's blindness was addressed by God's gracious work. We might suppose that if the man who had been healed had been asked if he had any residual resentment about having to wait for healing well into adulthood, he might have said: "It's all worth it! I'm so very grateful that I can see. The years seem like nothing!"

The question about the purpose(s) of suffering continues to be asked: "Why this, why me, why now?" but there are many reasons why God brings suffering into our lives.

Certainly, the man's blindness, mentioned above, was an occasion for a display of the power of God to heal and to restore. Whenever that kind of healing of someone who has been ill takes place, it stands as a remarkable testimony to the power of God. When God intervenes after the efforts of the best minds and the best medicines have failed to effect a cure, we are (or should be) amazed at the grace and power of God. We should praise and glorify God.

Most often, however, God does not bring about healing in that way; the suffering individual continues to suffer. Instead, God gives a measure of his sustaining grace so that the believing sufferer is able to continue pursuing a limited schedule, continuing to function as a parent or spouse, continuing to do whatever God has called him or her to do. We can think immediately of the apostle Paul who prayed three times for God to remove the thorn in his flesh. Aside from what we may believe that the thorn was, we understand that Paul believed he was hindered in conducting the ministry to which God had called him. Much to his sanctified delight, the very source of his irritation proved to be a cause for his realizing the sustaining grace of God. God said essentially, "No." "My grace is sufficient for you for my power is made perfect in weakness."[3]

The apostle Paul received God's sustaining grace, which served more to bring glory to God. It is truly a blessing and spiritual encouragement to Christians when God provides sustaining grace for people of faith into whose lives he has brought chronic suffering. Those believers who experience that kind of trial are often more joyful, more gracious, more tenderhearted, more characterized by peace than those who have no obvious afflictions. God is to be glorified because of the work he is performing in the lives of such individuals. He is shaping them and forming Christ in them. We can be encouraged in our faith through the exemplary suffering of others.

What's more, sickness and suffering refine and reform the ones who suffer. They are agents for the sufferer's spiritual benefit. Let's not forget what Jesus did not say. He answered a specific question from his disciples about the specific cause of the man's blindness. He did not say that sin was not at all involved in the man's blindness. What he did say was that the man's blindness was not due immediately to particular sin(s) on his part or to sin(s) on the part of his parents; but sin was part of the picture.

The Bible is very clear about the origin of sickness, suffering and death. Humanity brought these upon itself. God, who is the source and sustainer of all life, created man good and in his own image.[4] "God created man, male and female, in his own image and in knowledge, righteousness, and holiness, to rule over the other creatures; [but] left to the freedom of their own wills, our first parents sinned against God and fell from their original condition."[5] The Bible points out the significance of what our first parents did in Eden. It says: " ... sin came into the world through one man, and death through sin, and so death spread to all men, because all sinned."[6] The Westminster Shorter Catechism summarizes the consequences of sin and describes the misery of man's fallen condition: "By their fall, all mankind lost fellowship with God and brought his anger and curse on themselves. They are therefore subject to all the miseries of this life, to death itself, and to the pains of hell forever."[7] God isn't responsible for the mess people find themselves in. He created people forever to be well and productive. The first man was given a command, obligated to obey it and warned what would happen if he did not.[8] When put to the test, man defected and brought the guilt and misery of sin upon himself and all his descendants. Mankind fell into a state of sin and misery.

John Calvin said this about illnesses: "[They] serve ... us as medicine to purge us from worldly affections, and retrench what is superfluous in us, and since they are to us the messengers of death, we ought to learn to have one foot raised to take our departure when it shall please God."[9]

"Sickness helps to remind us of death. Most people live as if they were never going to die. They [pursue] business, or pleasure, or politics, or science as if earth was [sic] their eternal home. They plan and scheme for the future, like the rich fool in the parable (Luke 12:15-21), as if they had a long lease of life, and were not simply short-term tenants. A heavy illness goes far to dispel these delusions. It awakens us from our day-dreams, and reminds us that we have to die as well as to live."[10]

I'm not suggesting that sickness is good; anything that comes about as a result of the fall of mankind into sin is not good, but God does use all things for his glory and for the spiritual good of those who love him.[11]

Another spiritually beneficial result of sickness is that the sufferer is drawn closer to God. The suffering of sickness frequently opens the spiritual eyes of the afflicted. King David declared: "It is good for me that I was afflicted that I might learn your statutes."[12] Isn't it your experience that when you go through a serious illness that you wonder what God is trying to tell you? You ask yourself if you have committed any sin for which you are being punished. Your thoughts are turned to what you know you should be doing and away from what you know that you should not be doing. Suffering gets our attention and directs it to God.

Yet another benefit is that God uses sickness to correct and discipline his own people. Again, King David discovered that affliction can often lead us to God's Word. "Before I was afflicted I went astray, but now I keep your word."[13] Sometimes God uses affliction as a corrective. When a Christian is engaged in practices that are clearly not God's will, God may bring sickness into that person's life as a temporal judgment and as an agent to bring that sinful practice to an end. King Uzziah is regarded as one of the "good" kings of Judah, but there came a time when he became proud and unfaithful to God. He presumed to exercise the prerogatives of the Levitical priesthood and God afflicted him with leprosy. He had to live out his life in isolation, separated from his family and friends and the people over whom he reigned.[14]

Then too, God uses our suffering to cause us to *experience* that he is the God of great comfort. The apostle Paul referred to God as the Father of all mercies and the God of all comforts.[15] God comforts *his* people in all their afflictions. It is in and through the afflictions we suffer that God proves to us that he is the great comforter. God shows us that he is able to relieve and strengthen us, that he upholds us in our greatest distresses. We come to know God's comforting grace experientially.

Part of the benefit of suffering involves God's equipping us to minister to others. After we have received God's comfort – and many, many times during – we can sympathize with and extend the very comfort God has granted to us to others who, like us, suffer a variety of afflictions. We become more sensitive to the hurt and pain of others after we have suffered. It is as though we may take some of the very comfort we have received and share it with others. In all of these ways God will use the sufferings his people endure to form Christ in them, to make them more like Christ.[16] We know that Christ understands our suffering because he is the supreme sufferer. Since Christ suffered in principle what his people suffer, we who are his people can and should come to him to receive his grace and help in our time of need.[17]

These are just a few of the reasons that God brings suffering into our lives. You do not know the answers to *all* the "why" questions, but you can know the answers to many of them from the Word of God. In view of what God has made clear in his word, it is not well that we should ask questions like: "Why this?" Why not this? Would something else achieve God's purpose for you? "Why now?" Why not now? From a strictly human standpoint, is there ever a good time for suffering? "Why me?" Why not you? No one on the planet is immune from crushing sorrow. If you actually knew the answers to the "why" questions, would it make a difference in your condition? And, what if you were to disagree about God's purpose? Could you change it? The Bible is filled with examples of godly responses to suffering. They are included to teach us so that we may have hope.[18]

It is natural to ask the "why" questions at a time of great loss, but perhaps better questions would be the "what" questions. Try as best you can to discover "what" God would have you do at this time. Ask "what" it is that he expects of me in my situation. Ask "how" questions; not "How could God allow something like this," but "How may I honor and glorify God in these circumstances; how may I bear a faithful witness to the grace of God in my life at this time; how may I be an example for others to imitate when they are faced with similar situations?"

So very often those who are going through crisis or severe suffering will comment to others or reassure themselves that there must be a reason for it. We may hear people express sentiments like this: "There must be a purpose and though I don't know the purpose now, I will understand it in days ahead." Once again, the Bible informs us of many reasons that we undergo sufferings, and therefore, we are not totally confused about them. We do not need to wait for some time in the future to comprehend what God is doing with us or in us now. We live in a world where suffering is part of everyone's experience. There simply are no exceptions! Those who believe that Christ came to put an ultimate end to all suffering for his people understand that temporal suffering is a sanctifying, transforming agent. We know what God is bringing about through difficulties of suffering. That knowledge does not diminish them, but God grants his grace to all who ask it of him.

In my personal reading I have come across a statement by the late James Montgomery Boice, which gives perspective on the entire matter of suffering. I appreciate what he said to those who were concerned about him during his illness and I have included his helpful comments at this juncture.

A number of you have asked what you can do for me in my illness. You can do what you are doing, which is to pray. For what should you pray? Should you pray for a miracle? Well, you're free to do that, of course. My general impression is that the God who is able to do miracles – and he certainly can – is also able to keep one from getting the problem in the first place. So although miracles do happen, they're rare by definition. A miracle has to be an unusual thing. I think it's far more profitable to pray for wisdom for the doctors and then also for the effectiveness of the treatment.

Above all, I would say pray for the glory of God. If you think of God glorifying himself in history and you say, "Where in all of history has God most glorified himself?" he did it at the cross of Jesus Christ, and it wasn't by delivering Jesus from the cross, though he could have. Jesus said, "Don't you think I could call down from my Father ten legions of angels for my defense?" But he didn't do that. And yet that's where God is most glorified.

If I were to reflect on what goes on theologically here, there are two things I would stress. One is the sovereignty of God. That's not novel. I have always talked about the sovereignty of God. God is in charge. When things like this come into our lives, they are not accidental. It's not as if God somehow forgot what was going on, and something bad slipped by. God does everything according to his will.

But what I've been impressed with mostly is something in addition to that. It's possible, isn't it, to conceive of God as sovereign and yet indifferent? God's in charge but he doesn't care. But it's not that. God is not only the one who is in charge; God is also good. Everything he does is good. And what Romans 12:1-2 says is that we have the opportunity by the renewal of our minds – that is, how we think about things – actually to prove what God's will is. And then it says, "His good, pleasing, and perfect will" (NIV).

Is that will good, pleasing, and perfect to God? Yes, of course, but the point of it is that it's good, pleasing, and perfect to us. If God does something in your life, would you change it? If you'd change it, you'd make it worse. It wouldn't be as good. So that's the way we want to accept it and move forward.19

The knowledge of God's greatness *"gives comfort to all who are in the midst of trials, temptations, or sorrow.* Temptations and sorrows do come, as we know. They come to Christians and non-Christians alike. The question is: how shall we meet them? Clearly, if we must face them with no clear certainty that they are controlled by God and are permitted only for his own good purposes, then they are meaningless and life is a tragedy. On the other hand, if God is still in control, then these circumstances are known to him and have their purpose."[20]

Chemo Treatments

On a routine basis, Grace went to the oncology offices to undergo chemo treatment and to receive other infusions to promote her health. I would accompany her. There would be a standard questionnaire at the onset of the visit, a physical exam, and a doctor's consultation prior to the treatments. It was well that I went with her simply to remind her and **the doctors** of her health changes since previous treatments. The nurses had access to the "vitals" of the previous visit, but I had these as well and asked questions about changes in the numbers that had not occurred to Grace. It was helpful in getting responses to those questions if only to gain a better understanding of the bigger picture.

If you are caring for your wife in a similar situation, *keep your own records.* Ask the technicians and nurses for the numbers of the various readings that they take. When you are at home and think of questions about the process or the effects of the treatments, write them down so you will be ready to ask the physician about your concerns at the time of your wife's next appointment. Ask questions; the doctors shouldn't object; they are working **for** you and your wife. In fact, most doctors welcome questions. Your questions indicate a level of involvement in the treatment of your wife. You need, if at all possible, to go with your wife to these appointments. You are supporting her on many levels when you do. Be involved with your wife's care in this area as well; don't let her go it alone. You are dealing with and experiencing her last illness together. Be involved in as many ways as you can. Give her the support and understanding you would want from her if your roles were reversed. Even if you think you would not want that kind of involvement from her, she wants it from you!

After the consultation we (she) would be escorted to a large room where several people were receiving various chemical treatments for a variety of cancers. In combination with the serum was a sedative which further relaxed the patients. It was not unusual for a number of them to fall asleep while they received their chemo treatments. Each patient was seated in a large, adjustable chair and aids made sure that the patients were as comfortable as possible. Pillows and foot rests added comfort. Because the drugs or infusions often made patients chilly, each patient received a heated blanket. The treatment was begun.

At the early visits to the treatment center, I was surprised at how varied the clientele was. Adults of all ages, sizes, shapes and ethnicities were receiving medication. The facility we used was not one that accommodated children. The patients' cancers were in various stages. Some people appeared strong and otherwise healthy, others seemed worn and listless, but all had one thing in common: cancer had intruded into their lives and they had chosen to alter their routine in an attempt to extend or to save their lives. Grace would take her place among the group and while I read; she would close her eyes and rest or fall asleep. Treatment would run from two to four hours depending on a variety of factors. The nurses would be able to give us a rough idea of how long we would be "in today". Sometimes, I would leave to do household chores or shopping, but I would always return in time to be there for the end of her treatment.

I must say that the staff at the oncology center was highly specialized, experienced, caring and professional in every sense of the word. The personnel knew their work and did it well! I thank God for that facility and thousands like them across the country. I thank him that we live at a time and in a setting where such exceptional medical treatment is available and that Grace could take advantage of it. I am reminded that God has determined where people live as well as the length of their lives.[21] He places us into a complex context and gives us ample opportunity to seek him.

During the last couple of years of Grace's life, we were able to function fairly normally. We did all the things that people do who are not facing cancer together. We took short vacations, tended to housekeeping chores, made meals together, ran errands and attended gatherings. At that point, Grace was still able to attend worship and other activities, but everything wearied her. As time went on however, more and more of her life and mine was given to managing her health and going to appointments for various consultations and treatments. Just the same, we took the time to go on little outings.

On one such occasion we went to a nearby shopping mall to pick up a few things. Grace was standing near me looking at some of the merchandise when she fainted. It was all I could do to catch her and guide her collapse to the floor. I called for help but no one responded. People just looked on from a distance. I tried to bring Grace back to consciousness by calling her name and gently shaking her. In a few moments – what seemed much longer – she regained consciousness and was able to sit on the floor. She said, "I don't know what happened! I felt dizzy and then went blank." As she attempted to stand up, she fainted again and I called out again. This time the store manager came with a glass of water. After a few moments, Grace revived and sat still on the floor, drank a little water and was able to take a few nibbles of a cookie someone had offered. When she was able to stand safely, the store manager asked if she were sufficiently strong to walk. She was. So, he walked with us out of the store premises, through the mall to the exit. I think the experience was more frightening for me than for Grace. I didn't know what might have been going on inside her. Her health had become so delicate. We returned home and Grace just rested the remainder of the day. Future outings were greatly limited. This event was part of my wife's gradual decline, one of the many episodes that signaled her increasingly weakening condition.

At this point in our experience, I routinely did the grocery shopping alone, but on rare occasions she was able to join me. Grace would hold onto the shopping cart for support and slowly we would make our way through the aisles. She wasn't able to do an entire shopping, and often asked me to take her to a resting area where she waited until I gathered the groceries. When she could, she accompanied me on other errands, but remained in the car while I did the footwork. She basically went along for the ride, but at least we were together. I should have realized that these would be among our last outings.

Chapter Three

Wife's Decline

For I know the plans I have for you, declares the LORD, plans for welfare and not for evil, to give you a future and a hope. (Jeremiah 29:11)

During the final month of Grace's stay in the hospital, I kept track of what medications she took, who visited, and what and when she ate – if she ate at all. I attended to her physical needs much of the time, but as opportunity provided I prayed with and for her and read to her. Sometimes we would just be silent together. We came to know several of the staff nurses and over the days and weeks, could piece together their "stories". I became a familiar face to those at the nurses' station, security personnel, and coffee shop employees. After several days, I had learned the short-cuts of navigating through the hospital maze, using the back stairs and staff routes to get in and out of the hospital more easily.

Grace had been in the hospital for a month when, on Christmas Eve, she was discharged. I believed it was simply a Christmas courtesy. It was clear to me that the medical staff knew how ill my wife was but wanted to see her home for what would be her last Christmas. We both read the discharge papers and noted a comment made by an internist: "High risk of return". That was certainly an understatement!

So we were home for Christmas. We couldn't go anywhere or have any visitors. Grace just lay on the couch. I had set up a large coffee table near the couch's edge on which to place her vitamins and meds, and where I would bring the meager meals I brought to her. We just sat and talked. Grace rarely left the couch. Earlier in the summer she had fallen in the kitchen and broken her right arm. Due in large part to her weakened recuperative powers, her arm did not heal well. She lay on her back or on her left side the entire duration of her home and hospice care. We really did not "do" Christmas at that time.

Grace did return to the hospital within a couple of weeks. Big hugs and welcoming smiles from the nursing staff greeted her. The nurses knew her story and the routine that had stopped on Christmas Eve essentially resumed. After ten days, Grace was again released from the hospital to return home and at that time, *she* determined that she would not re-enter the hospital. "Let God bring about what he will," she said. "I want to die at home."

She was discharged with instructions for her care and a list of medications and supplements, some of which she was allowed to take with her from the hospital. When we arrived home, I helped her upstairs and she resumed her position on the couch. I again positioned the coffee table near the edge of the couch as a surface on which to place her food and meds. Together, we talked through the order and timing of her taking the various medications she was given. Some of them couldn't be taken with food, others required a specific time of day, and still others could not be taken in conjunction with certain drugs. We didn't want her to schedule anything for which she had to be awakened from a sound sleep. We plodded through a rigorous routine of pill-taking for a couple of weeks until Grace could no longer get some of the meds down. Her appetite declined markedly during this time as well.

As the weeks wore on and Grace became virtually helpless, she would say: "I feel so useless. I am helpless and useless. I am such a burden to you; I just want to be done with this life."

For someone who had been so very "hands-on" she had become a virtual nonparticipant in life. Perhaps it was difficult for her to recall that one's worth is not determined or decided by what one can do. One's worth is determined by God who created men and women as his image-bearers. He has further demonstrated his love for them by sending his Son to die for his people. He gives physical and spiritual life, and not because of anything they have done, are doing, or will do. One's worth is determined by God and not by the utilitarian value assigned by society.

The dying have worth because they are image-bearers of God and because they are God's agents of sanctification in the lives of those who love them and care for them. Family members are drawn to prayer as are friends and members of the churches to which they belong. Those individuals learn to pray for understanding, patience, strength and peace. They learn about the sovereignty of God in real time. These suffering struggling women are loved by their husbands, children and grandchildren. They are loved by the members of the extended family, the church members, and they are the concern of caring neighbors. Many people are touched by the sufferings of one. The connectedness of a caring community reaches far.

Near the end of Grace's life, her physical decline was rapid. At the start of her last six months, she could stand by herself, walk slowly by herself, dress herself and take care of personal hygiene; but a few months later she required help standing up. Toward the end of her hospital stay, when she was strong enough, I would help her out of the bed. She would take my arm and we would very slowly walk the distance of the hallway. Sometimes she wouldn't make it very far down the hall, and say simply, "I need to go back."

It was not long before Grace could not take care of herself in any respect. While she was in hospice, arrangements were made for a couple of LPN's to help with her personal and private needs. On one occasion, I asked her if she would like an aid to stay with us and help her with these matters and she replied, "I wouldn't want anybody doing what you are doing. We'll do the best we can." Eventually we declined further LPN assistance.

She also commented on the loss of her dignity: "You know, I've always been proper; I've always tried to be a proper English woman. Now look at me! This is degrading! There's no dignity, no personal privacy." There was no personal privacy – not in a hospital, not in home hospice. That reality in itself was a great personal loss. Grace said it was humiliating but knew those personal and private things had to be done. She wanted me to take care of her rather than to have someone else do it. Grace could not help herself at all; her sense of personal dignity was gone. That loss, plus the increasing loss of ability to do other physical things deepened her depression and sorrow.

But the physical is not the only area in which loss takes place. If your wife has memory loss or has developed another kind of mental limitation, she is experiencing loss that she perhaps does not understand. It is as real a loss as that of a physical ability, or of speech or sight or mobility. As you witness what your wife is losing mentally, you share her sorrow. It is a loss for you as well. As her physical and mental capacities diminish, you experience a kind of loneliness even while she is with you. This is part of what you may expect to go through. I encourage you to recognize this aspect of caring for your wife. Be gracious as you minister to her changing and increasing needs. I would simply say to those who visit friends or family in such a physical or mental condition to remember that they are visiting people who have lost so much. They have forgone pride; they've lost independence even for private matters and there is that feeling of the loss of dignity. Those who minister to people in that state must remember that those whom they serve have lost so much more than physical ability alone. When the loss of life happens slowly, what makes up much of living is lost slowly as well. In a very real sense, one who dies in this way mourns his or her own death before it occurs, and so do those who care for them. Some have come to call this grief anticipatory grief.[1] A pall of sorrow fills the room of those who die slowly; the dying mourn with those who love them. They mourn their own deaths and feel sorrow for what those who are left behind will face without them.

Those who die slowly experience tremendous losses – loss of independence, loss of abilities, loss of privacy, loss of opportunities of living what might have been a longer and certainly a more enjoyable life. The husbands who serve as caregivers for their dying wives deal with the grieving and share in that sorrow constantly. If you wish to minister to a man who is experiencing this, you might acknowledge the losses that he and his wife share. It might prove to be a kindness to recognize this aspect of his experience, and whereas you can't "understand," you can acknowledge that you don't understand. You know simply that there is the sadness of increasing loss. You might pray with and for that man who cares for his dying wife about those very concerns.

I was still employed full-time when my wife's health took an obvious turn downward. I still was expected to perform my responsibilities, carrying out my duties regardless of Grace's condition. I continued to do my work *as if* things were normal. Consequently, sometimes friends would voice their concern that I was holding any expressions of my feelings deep inside: "Why aren't you more concerned?" "Why" they wondered *aloud*, "don't you express more sorrow; why do you seem to be able to go on as if nothing were wrong?" I suppose that I had not exhibited an expected pattern of acceptable mourning. Perhaps my composure was perceived as uncaring. Three things among others I'm sure, serve to answer those questions.

First, the illness that took the life of my wife was long-term. Her struggle was spread over fourteen years. In the depths of our hearts we knew, that barring a miraculous healing by God, she would eventually succumb to the cancer. The initial diagnosis had been a numbing shock to both of us. It was like a dark and dreaded hall into which we knew we would walk together. The psalmist called it the "Valley of the Shadow of Death".[2] Our grieving and sadness extended well over a decade. I understand that such is not the case for many couples who go through a terminal illness. The time between diagnosis and death may be extremely brief for them. When death occurs in a briefer timeframe, men are astonished at the unexpectedness of their wives' deaths.

Some interviewees experienced the *rapid* decline of their wives and expressed their shock or surprise:

Once Heather started getting sick there was a daily decline in her mental health and in her physical status. We moved [to an area where we could receive specialized medical attention. Near] . . . the end, she could not eat or talk or walk. Two weeks before her death due to some innovative medical treatments, she was just about back to normal. [So] this major decline was such a surprise. I fully expected her to get better. I didn't believe she would pass as soon as she did. It was a total surprise. ZB

One day getting ready for work Tammy couldn't get her breath and [so] . . . I took her to the emergency [facility] where her pulmonologist was. They were going to do a test the next day [but] she had cardiac arrest twice before they could do the test. She was basically unconscious in the ICU for the next few days . . . three days later . . . she passed. It was all very much of a shock. WZ

Yes, I was surprised because Sharon was very healthy and took good care of herself. She was very conscientious about eating habits. This caught everybody by surprise. They found cancer in a random x-ray. AM

It was totally unexpected. From when she was diagnosed to her passing it was not longer than 45 days... [W]hen she went into the intensive [care]... there was always hope. We had no idea that she had [this condition] and there was always the hope that she would recuperate, that she'd recover. For twenty or twenty-five of the [next] thirty days, she was in intensive care. There were two brain operations to relieve the pressure on her head and the doctors never really said, "There's not a chance of recovery," and so we sat there [in the waiting room] waiting hopefully for some good news but it didn't come. RP

When some couples realize what will soon take place, their emotions come flooding over them like the waters of a ruptured dyke. Expressions of emotions are sometimes explosive! But, it was not the case with us. Our faith in God helped us immeasurably, or perhaps better, the God in whom we had faith helped us immeasurably. His word explains that he does us no evil. Everything that takes place in the lives of his children happens for their ultimate spiritual good.[3] We were thoroughly convinced of this! This perspective is not a resignation to fate; it is the reality of faith. The God who has loved us to such an extent to send his Son to die on our behalf will not ever change his mind about us. We were convinced, and I remain convinced that our God does only what is right.

A second reason for the (apparent) composure in this crisis is that practically speaking, during the last year of my wife's life I was already functioning as a single person. Things we had done together – shopping, meal preparation, housecleaning, errand running, and even church life – I had come to do *as* a single person. Things Grace had done – home administration, banking, laundry, taxes, health care tracking, business, etc.

– I *gradually* assumed. She was there during that transition to answer particular questions I had but basically, I had assumed all the responsibilities for the things I previously had done just occasionally. Many of the changes in sharing the household responsibilities, the cooperation and comradery, came about prior to my wife's passing. That prepared me better for the responsibilities I would have later. That last year before Grace died was a mercy itself. It was a time of preparation and transition for me to live the life I would have later. God granted mercy to me to allow me to ease into new roles and responsibilities. Many of the changes I would need to make; many of the responsibilities I would need to assume were made and assumed prior to my wife's passing. It was a blessing in having a prolonged transition time. I did not view that period as an extended misery. No! It was an opportunity to do things and say things that a shorter period of time or a sudden death would not have allowed.

Perhaps a third reason was that I had been brought up not to show emotion. I did not grow up with the freedom to express my feelings. "Keep it to yourself" was the prevalent approach to what was going on in the heart. Part of the home and community culture that was mine involved being stoic and stolid. I just learned to keep things inside. I might add that I had pastoral responsibilities during much of the time of my wife's illness; and whereas I did not serve like an Old Testament priest, I was reminded by the Scripture that a high priest who served was not permitted to show any grief even if his parents were to die.[4] The prophet Ezekiel as well, in his unique ministry, was told that his wife would die and that he was not to mourn her. Certainly, when his wife died, he was sorrowful and grieved, but he was not permitted to mourn in the customary way.[5] These are special cases where the roles those individuals played disallowed a display of their grief. Those closest to me knew that I kept the range of the expression of my emotions within very narrow margins. This "keep-it-inside" approach is common for men.

Time of Transition

There usually is a division of labors in a marriage. Over the years marriage partners specialize in doing the work of making the marriage and operating a home a success. Day-to-day administration has been parsed to make for a smooth running of the household and family. When the wife dies, one of the "specialists" is gone. Grace was exceptional when it came to math. She managed our banking. She had become well-acquainted with tax laws and took care of our tax obligations on a local, state and federal level. She secured insurance for our material goods and for our health. She was the custodian of the coupons, and knew when and where to look for sales. These were her "areas".

While men who experience the sudden deaths of their wives may not have taken the opportunity to discuss practical matters of this sort, those whose wives face a slow yet inevitable death have an opportunity to speak with their wives about these very down-to-earth concerns. They will have to learn to deal with them. Dealing with finances, insurance, legal matters and others becomes part of the sadness of their loss that will need to be placed on the table for frank discussion. Conversations about these matters might not be so cumbersome, but the situation that calls for discussing them at this time brings urgency and the sadness into the moment. Some husbands have a hard time taking up the responsibilities of administration that their wives seemed to have performed so effortlessly.

If you are anticipating the loss of your wife due to a long-term illness, you will experience many related emotional, physical and spiritual tests. Those of you walking with your wives through their slow deaths may discover that in certain respects, the adjustment to your new status was not as difficult as you had expected. Even if you have already begun to make that adjustment, matters other than the mechanics of daily living will press upon you. In chapters that follow, I will address concerns of loneliness, the physical and emotional side of loss, and some of the social aspects of being newly widowed.

Be assured of this: God will not forget about you. You can trust in him under all circumstances and in all conditions. At times it may seem to you that God is distant and not concerned for what you suffer, but what may seem to be, is not. God is with his people always. He will never leave or forsake them, but more, he is present to counsel, to comfort and to console them. God never said, "No" to prayers his people pray to him for help. In his wisdom and plan, he may not grant precisely what they request, but he always offers his grace and peace to them. If you have never approached God for his help, wouldn't now, during the present difficulties be the perfect time. As long as you live it is the perfect time to come to him.

Chapter Four

Time Together

Do not be anxious about anything, but in everything by prayer and supplication with thanksgiving let your requests be made known to God. And the peace of God, which surpasses all understanding, will guard your hearts and minds in Christ Jesus. (Philippians4:6-7)

After Grace was home from the hospital, there was not always a flurry of activity. In fact, at times, the hands on the clock seemed hardly to move. Much of the time passed with a sense of waiting. Certainly, Grace and I prayed together and I read the Bible to her. We discussed our situation and did engage in reminiscing, but there were also large blocks of time when I read to her on subjects of her interest. We both enjoyed the various mystery series offered on public television. Grace was fond of the Agatha Christie mysteries, especially the sleuthing of the fictional characters Miss Marple and Hercule Poirot. So, I purchased a couple volumes: *Miss Marple: The Complete Short Stories,* and *Masterpieces of Mystery and The Unknown*, and read several chapters to her each day. I had begun this practice before Grace's first hospitalization, continued to read to her both at home and in the hospital, through all of our remaining time together. Though she was partial to Agatha Christie's work, Grace also liked the various Sherlock Holmes adventures. I read much of Sir Arthur Conan Doyle's works to her. Hearing me read seemed to relax her and to distract her from her discomfort.

Discussions

In the hours you spend with your wife, you may have the opportunity to talk with her about her funeral. You should, if at all possible, have this discussion. Decisions *will* be made. Perhaps your wife will not want to talk about the matter but you should give her the opportunity to express her wishes. In fact, these kinds of discussion should not wait for one or both of you to be ill or near death. They should take place while both of you are younger and in good health.

One character in Bible history was very specific about his last wishes. I have Joseph in mind. When he was about to die, he gave instructions concerning the disposition of his body. He stipulated that when God would fulfill his promises to his people to give them the Promised Land, they would take his bones and bury them in that land rather than to have him interred in Egypt.[1] When the Israelites finally were delivered from their slavery to the Egyptians, Moses made sure to take Joseph's remains and a generation later, Joshua saw to it that Joseph's last wishes were carried out.[2] Perhaps this is in part where we get a cue to honor the last requests of dying friends and relatives. They express their desires to have certain things happen, their possessions dispersed in certain ways and certain things to happen to them. We try to honor that if we can – what items of clothing or jewelry should go to whom, who should receive the silverware or china or a favorite book. Grace had said to me more than once, "I don't want to be buried hundreds of miles from you or any of my children. I don't want a grave that's simply abandoned after I'm put in it."

Unlike two generations ago, today's extended family is not frequently situated in one town or district where members see one another on a regular basis. In the past, many families had sections of cemeteries purchased for the burial of family members. My great-grandmother, for example, had purchased a rather large area which included several burial plots for her children and grandchildren and even great grandchildren. Members of the extended family took turns tending the grave sites. Since our children were located in different parts of the country, my wife's request was all but impossible to fulfil. My anticipated move to live near my daughter made it possible to honor part of that request. My wife was buried within three miles of where I and my daughter currently live.

Wife's Questions

During another discussion with Grace about days ahead and my life without her, she asked me three very difficult questions. They may have *seemed* easy for her to ask but difficult for me to answer: "Do you want me to die?" and "Can you help me die?" and "Will you marry again?"

I believe the question most difficult to answer was: "Do you want me to die?" I do not know what made her ask it. Certainly, I have to take into account that near the end of anyone's life, the brain may not be working as efficiently as it did when that person had good health. There was no simple way to answer her question. She asked it within a few days of her death. I had realized deep down in my soul that my wife would not recover from the cancer. I would sometimes wonder what life would be like without her. Perhaps she could sense that I was becoming physically and emotionally weary taking care of her day and night. Not only had I been her primary caregiver, but during her last few weeks, I was her sole caregiver. Perhaps she could see that I was tiring. Maybe she supposed that I just wanted an end to all the difficulties we had recently faced together. I don't know. I admit to thoughts that life, in many respects, would be less difficult for me and certainly more beneficial for her if she were to die. Grace's death would bring relief and release. It would bring sorrow and deep grief, but it would also bring relief. How could I answer a pointed question like the one she asked? I could not reply with a straightforward "Yes" and I could not – in her current condition – honestly say "No", but I wanted to be as encouraging, as helpful and as faithful to her as I possibly could be, right up to the very end.

Some of the interviewees express a sense of release and relief upon the deaths of their wives.

In some ways, her death would be a relief for both of us. Certainly, others have thought along these lines when they have considered the pain and the suffering of their dying loved one. I didn't want her to suffer anymore, but . . . Yes, I was relieved though I didn't want to lose her. AM

Yes I was relieved. There was a great weight was lifted off of me. At that point [in time] the burden I was carrying was trying to maintain a household on my own. That was a lot to carry and when [Lindsey] died, yes, I sat down a wept, but it didn't last long. My heart felt free for the first time in months. I don't understand how people can go through years of that [grieving] . . . For me it was anguish . . . but I knew that her days were quickly coming to an end. I was relieved for her that she was no longer suffering. She was [then] no longer dealing with pain and it was a relief to me that this chapter could actually have an end to it rather just go on and on and on. JA

There was some relief in that if the tables were switched, I think Tammy would have had a more difficult time practically speaking, just dealing with everyday stuff . . . So I was glad of that. [If I had died] it would have been worse, not because of my death, but because her burden. WZ

My wife and I had open conversations about her death. We discussed how the family should be told, funeral arrangements, burial, my future without her, etc. We had spoken freely about our faith in God's goodness and his love for us, and that, whereas God had the power to heal her completely, it appeared that for his divine purposes, he would not do so. So, when my wife asked me: "Do you want me to die?" I answered something like this: "I would like you to be strong again; to be free of this terrible disease. I would like you to get better and be healthy as you were before, but it seems that God is going to take you to himself very soon. It will be loss and heavy sadness for me but peace and joy for you. I will continue to pray that God would give you his mercy and ease your suffering." She seemed satisfied with that answer. She was just quiet when I spoke the words. A few moments later she fell asleep.

During the last month of my wife's life she was in hospice care. Grace and I chose to use the services of home hospice care after several days of discussing the upsides and downsides of such a choice (See Hospice Care in chapter five). One of my concerns about facing her death was the legal aspect. Usually when someone dies at home, there is some inquiry as to the circumstances of that death. In some cases an autopsy is performed. I wondered if I would have to call paramedics or if having called them they would try to revive my wife – something Grace clearly did not want. We had posted a sign in an obvious place where anyone coming into our home would see the "Do Not Resuscitate" document. Neither of us wanted her to be brought back to the hospital against her expressed wishes.

When we were considering hospice care one of our questions for the social workers was, "Will there be a requirement to call paramedics, or a doctor, or the hospital?" The clear answer was in a word, "No". A physician must *recommend* hospice care; the physician and the dying patient (or one who has the power to make a decision) must come to an agreement that further medical treatment would be pointless, and that the best thing to do would be to make a dying person as comfortable as possible. In the state where we lived at the time, the death of someone in hospice care is expected. There would be no paramedics or last hospital stay and there would be no autopsy. That is exactly what my wife wanted. A hospice nurse with the authority to pronounce time of death would be the only person involved. The nurse would then call the funeralist with whom prior arrangements had been made.

I say all this by way of explanation and background for the second question my wife asked me. Again, I do not know the condition of her mind, nor can I explain her thinking process, but she knew there would be no autopsy. So she asked me in a moment of stress and depression, "Can you help me die? Can you just put a pillow over my face; it wouldn't take very long and I would be done with the suffering?" I was stunned and saddened to hear her words! Again, I was reminded in just another way of the suffering my wife was going through, how she wanted it to end and how desperately she wanted to "go home".

Grace confided to me on some mornings that she had been awake most of the night praying that the Lord would take her. There were times when she expressed disappointment and even of frustration in the fact that she had to face another day. She admitted that she had her moments of being upset with God because he would not answer her prayer for death. I tried to assure her that God had a precise time for her and as much as she didn't like it, she would have to wait.

I believe that Grace, in her more lucid moments, would not have asked her second question. In her mind she was done with this life, and wanted to go to heaven. In her healthier days she had very strongly expressed her opinion about suicide and assisted death. She wanted life promoted; her view was very theologically informed. I was surprised that she spoke the words: "Will you help me die?" She actually had thought of a way for me easily to help her!

My answer was as straightforward as her question had been. I said that I would not. God is the only one who can give life and it remains his divine prerogative to take it as he will and when he will. And, even though there would not be an autopsy, helping her die would be taking a life. Even if no one else would ever know, I would know. I would carry that weight for the rest of my life! And, God would know! Ultimately, I would have to answer to him. Once again, I assured my wife that I would pray for her and with her for God's mercies. I assured her that I would do all I could do to ease her pain and comfort her, but I would not take her life. Again she was silent; she knew I was right.

Euthanasia is an issue that some couples deal with near the end of the life of one of them. It's not my purpose in writing these thoughts to discuss that issue. The Bible states very clearly that the willful, premeditated ending of life is forbidden. The sixth Commandment, "You shall not kill," means actually, "You shall not murder". The word for "kill" is used of planned and deliberate action in taking another's life. It refers to the taking of human life only, not to the killing of animals or of humans during a time of war. It is used of the plotting that brought about the death of Naboth by Jezebel [and Ahab].[3] The matter of deliberately causing the death of someone although not immediately involved in the action, still brings the guilt of murder upon the one who planned the death.[4] In the case of David planning the death of Uriah the Hittite, this is very clear. King David never touched Uriah, but God's prophet Nathan declared that David had killed Uriah (caused him to be smitten).[5]

The Bible makes a clear distinction between premeditated killing and accidental, unintended manslaughter.[6] What we would call first degree murder and manslaughter are treated differently. The word of God made provisions for those who caused death but who had no intention of doing so. Euthanasia or "mercy killing" is as intentional as suicide. The Bible's teaching on this issue is sufficiently clear. The deliberate taking of another's life is as an assault of the image of God in man.[7] Every human being is an image-bearer of God. God alone gives life; no one else can create it. It is God's prerogative to give life and his to take it away when he sees fit.

There was a third question Grace asked and again it was as straightforward as the first two had been. I guess near the end of one's life there isn't time for easing gently into issues. So she asked, "Will you marry again?" I certainly didn't expect *that* question! Why would she ask that? Why would she care one way or another? Well, she was thinking of me as she explained when I made my reply. I said something like, "I don't think so; it's hard to start over." I expect that one could argue for or against remarriage and make a good case on either account. Remarriage, however, was not even on my radar screen! It just wasn't. I gave my wife some of my reasons why I thought that it would not be a good idea, and that I would not be seeking remarriage. You see, it could be argued on the one hand that a man unwilling to remarry had not thought very highly of the marriage institution, or on the other hand that he had thought so highly of his wife that no one would ever replace her, or had had such a difficult time in the marriage that he did not want to be married again. (See remarriage later in chapter eleven).

The reverend Al Martin related a similar exchange he had with his wife before she died.

In the weeks before her death, Marilyn, fully aware that she was dying, yet perfectly lucid in mind, spoke clearly to me regarding her desires for me after her death. She couched these desires in three straight-forward assertions and directives: 1) [She] had come to the settled conviction that God did not mean for me to be alone, but that in due course I should remarry . . . 2) I should not be bound by any man-made time frame for remaining a widower . . . [and] 3) in choosing another wife, I should not simply choose a worthy woman on some objective grounds. Rather, Marilyn's desire for me was that I would "fall madly in love.[8]

It interested me to realize that a number of men in the survey stated that they had had similar conversations with their wives, and that their wives had considered the possibility of their husband remarrying after their deaths.

I thought I was fine. It never even crossed my mind about remarriage until . . . about a year after Marla was gone. I can't explain it exactly, but there just seemed to be this tremendous sense of "missing". There just seemed to be this sense of incompletion and a void that started welling up in me. [For about three months the feeling] just grew; [it] just kept growing stronger and stronger and stronger . . . until finally. Finally, I got to the point . . . where I just got this sense that the Lord was giving me peace about [this] saying, "It's okay," to think in those terms [of remarriage]; that it may be that I needed someone else in my life. DM

"Would I want to be married?" . . . "Yeah." I mean I feel like I'm built for it [marriage] right now. It's the most uncomfortable feeling for a man that there is – because my best friend is gone. I was married and now I'm not; and I really want to be, but I don't let my heart think about that much. I know that [that would be] a dead-end street; there is no good way to end those thoughts. I cannot allow my mind to even speculate or imagine what it would be like to have a relationship with this person, [or] with that person. So as soon as I find myself thinking that way, that's when I really pray hard for the Lord to take that [thought] away from my heart, calm it down and to let me be at peace. [I want] to be content [and] to wait upon him. If any relationship happens, he's going to be the author of it. JA

I don't wish for my wife to be back. I'm glad she is where she is, but I am lonely for someone. I wish I could be married again. I was very near being remarried a couple of times. In fact, I asked someone to marry me but it didn't work out. There is someone else I would like to marry but things are difficult. LL

I had a close friend whom I knew for years. In fact, my wife had known of this individual and told me that I should marry her when she died. We had been in contact over the years and she knew of my situation. A couple of months after my wife died, we met and discussed the possibility of getting married. I asked her [to marry me] but she did not say "yes". We have broken off contact. I guess it's all for the best. At my age I cannot afford to waste a year or two courting someone only to find out that it has been a waste of time. I'm glad that the situation became clear sooner rather than later. I guess what another one of my friends told me is true. I guess I might have moved forward too soon. ZB

My wife was not convinced by any of my weak statements and inserted her opinion abruptly: "I want you to remarry. You need to be married. It would be good for you." I was as surprised by her forthright remarks as I had been by her question. I never thought she would say anything like that. My rejoinder was something like: "Well, I'm not going to seek remarriage. I won't be looking for another wife. If it happens, it'll happen in God's way and in God's time."

At the writing of this book, my view has changed only slightly. It is not as though I want to be married or that I am openly seeking marriage. I have prayed that God would continue to give me the grace to live as a single individual if that is indeed his will for me; and, that he would give me even more of his grace if he brought a wife into my life. I am not against remarriage as I initially opined to my dying wife.

Sadness

Sometimes between the conversations with my wife and the times of reading to her there would be silence – just silence. It seemed almost as though we needed silence. What we were experiencing together could not adequately be put into words and so we did not attempt to do so. Both of us could only imagine what the other was thinking but neither of us had the need to ask the other about private thoughts. These were times of personal reflection and we knew that we should not intrude upon the other's thoughts. Grace and I were married nearly forty-seven years and I was still surprised that much of our communication, especially then, was non-verbal. Occasionally Grace would break the silence, shake her head and say: "This is just so sad, so so sad," then look at me with a faraway look. I would respond with words of agreement, but also acknowledge that we had vowed to love each other in sickness and in health, in joy and in sorrow. I said this not only because it was true, but also to reassure her. This was part of the sickness and sorrow. It was sadness that we simply had to live with by the grace of God.

A Time to Plan

During the weeks of hospice, I had significant time for reflecting and preparing for the inevitable. My thoughts turned to the reality of being at my wife's funeral, but more, to the need to prepare her funeral. A funeral is among other things, a formal way to say "goodbye" and to review, if only in summary, the life of the loved one. Nobody wants to face that final "goodbye"; I certainly did not, so planning for it was not easy. If it could be said that there are any advantages to knowing that a loved one is going to die, having time to plan for the funeral event would be among them. Over the weeks that preceded her death, I listed possible Bible texts that could be used in the funeral service and songs that might be sung. I began to arrange the order of service.

My thoughts also turned to those whom I wanted to speak. All of us have attended funerals (See chapter eight below for additional thoughts on a funeral). We may wonder why certain elements were included and others left out. Some funerals that I have attended seemed unplanned and even confusing. My wife was a God-fearing woman. She loved the Lord and even as a young person had been involved in the ministries of the churches to which she had belonged. She was committed to the life and work of the church, but more, she was committed to the One whom she served in the church. I wanted a service for her that reflected her commitment to God, and his commitment to her. I had worked on a short biographical statement for the funeral bulletin, but also arranged the order of service, selecting three songs from several appropriate options. Shortly after the funeral was scheduled, I contacted those whom I wanted to speak at the service. I wanted them to prepare well, and they did.

The need to make these kinds of decisions quickly brings significant stress. Often grieving husbands receive help in making necessary choices. Some of the interviewees related how they felt having to make these kinds of decisions.

I really couldn't feel a thing. It was like I was under pressure to do many things very quickly. All my children came from various locations. They fixed up and cleaned the house and they did the entire funeral planning. ZB

My son took care of the funeral which I would usually have done. So that helped a lot. RP

Marla took care of all the funeral arrangements. I didn't need to do that because she had already done that unknown to me. She let me know about it . . . The funeral director that she was using had strict orders never to call our home after 4 o'clock because at that time I might be there. So, she had been doing [the arrangements] all the time. DM

I planned the funeral with the church folk. They had suggestions [about the use of] photographs. They had a checklist which helped in keeping things organized. I was able to walk through that process, but there were a lot of arrangements that I needed to do personally. WZ

During your wife's decline you will have time to be together. Make it quality time. The moments you share will be among your last together. Discuss your wife's wishes about her care. If you have children who can be involved at some level, bring them into some of the discussions with their mother. They understand that their mother is dying and will treasure opportunities to participate in her closing days. Plan as much as possible together. By the grace of God, do all you can to comfort and care for your wife.

Chapter Five

Hospice

Give strong drink to the one who is perishing, and wine to those in bitter distress; let them drink and forget their poverty and remember their misery no more. (Proverbs 31:6-7)

The interpretation of the verse I quoted is debated as both discouraging and encouraging the use of measures to reduce the suffering of the afflicted. In any case, people have used anodynes to lessen pain from time immemorial. The time came when my dear wife could no longer take oral medicine. I think the medical staff at both the hospital and the oncology center saw the signs of approaching death before I did. The hospital counselors and Grace's oncologist suggested that we consider hospice. Perhaps you will have a discussion about hospice care. If your wife's condition is showing no signs of reversal, you should have the discussion. Will a decision to use hospice care be viewed by family and friends as giving up the fight? How do you approach the subject? What place do the clergy have at this point, or members of your church? Will you want friends to visit you and your wife at home/hospice after that decision has been made? Is receiving visitors even an option?

In chapter four I had mentioned that my wife and I had chosen to use a hospice service during the last few weeks of her life. I thought it would be well to include some information about hospice care in the hope that it will give you a clearer basis for making a decision about the hospice approach to the end of the life of a loved one. After months of intense treatments and of being in and out of the hospital, Grace had reached her limit. She no longer wanted to be the object of cutting-edge technology or a trial specimen for the latest specialized medications. Clearly, for her medical efforts had been exhausted; there was no improvement in her condition and attempts to effect a halt to the cancer's incessant progress had failed. Aside from the fact that the cancer had already weakened her physically, the attempts to medicate her additionally wore her down physically and emotionally. She made it clear that she did not want to be placed in a nursing home or any other similar facility. She wanted to go home, period. She did not want any further medical interventions – period. She was done. She told me: "I want to die at home."

We did go home for the last six weeks of Grace's life. For about three weeks, we followed a rather rigid routine of taking medications and doing therapy, but as we sensed in each other, we knew that all of this would turn out to be pointless. One day Grace said to me, "Den, I want to stop the meds." I honestly do not remember how the discussion of hospice came up. Perhaps it was at the suggestion of her primary oncologist who provided the telephone number of someone we could call if we wanted to look into hospice. A friend of ours had lost her husband several years earlier. We did the best we could in maintaining a relationship with her afterward. Sometimes she and Grace would go for lunch, and sometimes Grace and I would stop by her home for a short visit. She and her late husband had determined to use hospice during his final days. Phyllis would occasionally comment to us about how pleased she was with the hospice care her husband had received in their home. She was glad that they had made the decision, and she gave us the clear impression that it had been the "right" thing for them to do. Her words certainly influenced our decision to use hospice care.

The time for our decision had arrived. I think it was Grace who started the conversation with a remark, "None of this is helping is it? I'm not getting better and I'm not going to get better." We discussed the hospice option and admitted that we did not know enough about it to make an informed decision. One of the concerns we had was how a decision to use hospice would be received by our children, by our church family, and by our many other praying friends. Would it appear as though we were abandoning hope in God; would it seem as though we were giving up; or, were we to take that step as part of God's will – as recognizing the obvious? To be sure, we prayed about this matter and had a sense of peace about our choice. For us this decision was more than an emotional hurdle, but we were convinced that, barring a miracle of divine intervention, Grace would die within a relatively short time. So, we sadly acknowledged this reality to one another and I made a call to have someone visit our home to inform us about hospice care. That decision was difficult but once we crossed the threshold to accept the reality of her death, we both were relieved. Let there be an end to the pains to save a life; let the time left be used to end her pain and bring a measure of physical comfort – pain from which Grace had had little relief for some time, and a comfort that had eluded her for months.

The general public is beginning better to understand the hospice concept. Hospice care offered a way to diminish Grace's pain so that her life could end peacefully. Though there was not a specific protocol question on the subject, over half of the men interviewed for this book mentioned the hospice care that their wives had received. Others perhaps took advantage of hospice services, but did not refer to them. These are samples of their comments about hospice.

Marla went into the hospital for that last time... she'd only been there for a couple of days until the doctors determined that it was time not to think in terms of cure but comfort and to going to a hospice situation. At first, she really struggled with that and I still remember her looking up at me and saying, "I can't give up," but she and I talked a lot about that and finally, you know, I was able to help her to come to the point where she could say, "No, I'm not giving up" . . . She finally did accept the fact that it didn't look like it was within God's will to heal her . . . She did not want to be in hospice over a long period of time. She found out that they also offered hospice in the facility that she was already in, so she asked, "Would you mind if I just stayed here for the hospice?" DM

Ruth and I knew that she would die seven months before she actually passed away. My wife agreed to enter hospice. She was actually one month and nine days in hospice. [She] and I were informed about a fourth chemo treatment that would eradicate the cancer or nearly kill the patient. At the time, we declined to have the treatment. Eventually, however, my wife agreed to have the fourth chemo treatment. When they did [it], it totally debilitated her. She was in the hospital for nearly two weeks trying to recover . . . I was surprised that her death came so soon after she entered hospice. She entered on [date] and five weeks later she was gone. LL

Carol had an unexpected aneurysm and was in intensive care thirty days. She went to hospice for about two weeks and then she passed away. RP

A nurse from the hospice [who] came to see her was checking out something. They had sensed a change in Lindsey's physical readings ... that indicated a downturn. It was something that meant the end is coming. JA

I made a call and scheduled an in-house appointment for a couple of days later. At that time a hospice nurse came and explained how hospice could work for us. Grace and I had generated several questions about the service, all of which the hospice nurse answered to our satisfaction. I was surprised to learn that with the particular hospice we were considering, people could choose to end hospice care because if significant improvement came about. Some people who had entered hospice care realized a wonderful return to health, to their amazement and to the amazement of their doctors. We were informed that once having left hospice, one could reenter it later when the need arose. All of this seemed extremely flexible for us. Grace's oncologist had anticipated our decision, so, after he received the report from the hospice worker, he granted his approval to hospice care without objection or delay.

At this point it might be helpful to offer a few specifics about hospice care generally. "Hospice care is for the dying. Its primary purpose is to work with the terminally ill and their families, to help them make the most of the time that's left, and to make their dying more comfortable, less frightening, and in every way more bearable."[1] "Today eighty-four percent of hospice patients nationally have cancer, and . . . the rest have a variety of other end-stage illnesses."[2] I will simply touch on four questions you may have about hospice: What is hospice; who is involved; where does it take place; and, what are the requirements for participation?

What is hospice?

Hospice "is a well-coordinated set of services intended to relieve or ease the various symptoms or side effects of a terminal illness. Many hospices are community-based agencies created just for this purpose, while others are departments or units of hospitals or home health agencies, although such hospice departments have the same specialized focus on care for the dying . . . Hospice services are directed by a physician and planned and provided by a team . . . of nurses, social workers, chaplains, therapists, personal care aides, and volunteers. Medical direction for the hospice team usually comes from the patient's primary physician, who in effect writes a prescription for hospice care, then reviews and authorizes the care the hospice provides."[3] As of this writing, Medicare requires two physicians to certify that a patient has six months or less to live, in order for a patient to receive Medicare benefits.

"In the United States hospice care has developed primarily as a program or a philosophy of care, not a place to go. A coordinated team of hospice workers generally will come to you and care for you in your own home, rather than you going to them. Hospice is committed to doing everything in its power to help dying patients remain in their homes, cared for by family and friends with the expert support of health professionals and volunteers, until they die."[4]

The hospice philosophy essentially proposes neither to hasten nor postpone death's advance; it is "instead to manage the patient's care as well as possible until the moment of death arrives."[5] Its goal is making dying patients as pain-free as possible, as comfortable and as active as possible, for as long as possible. "Hospice is carried out under the basic guidance of a written plan of care for each patient, developed by the team of hospice professionals with frequent input by telephone from the patient's doctor, who retains medical responsibility for patient's care."[6]

Who is involved?

As suggested above, hospice care is a team effort. It involves the primary care physician, and as was the case in my wife's situation, the oncologist; a case manager, a hospice nurse or nurses, social workers, personal care needs and technicians, and others, for example, a counselor or member of the clergy. These comprise a hospice team. They are in regular communication with one another; they read one another's reports so that there is a constant and agreed-upon approach for each patient. Observations, vital signs, and recommendations are documented and reviewed.

Where does hospice take place?

"Most of the time the care hospices provide is in the homes of dying patients, where the patient can be maintained in a more comfortable, familiar surroundings, attended by family and friends. This care is blended with the family's routine as much as possible. Hospice is not a place where patients go to die: it is a service that comes to wherever the patient is living."[7] The home care is intermittent; a member of the hospice staff is not with a patient all day or all night except in crises situations. Members of the hospice team pay regularly-scheduled visits to assess the patient's condition and needs, to answer the family's questions and to attend to any other concerns that have arisen since their last visit.

As noted above and as illustrated in an interviewee comment above (DM), some hospice organizations use various units in a hospital, which are designated for hospice use. Others may be situated in distinct facilities throughout the communities they serve.

What are the requirements for participations?

Requirements vary from state to state and sometimes from county to county, but generally, people who wish to take advantage of hospice care must meet six requirements.

The *first* requirement is that a person under medical care "has been given a medical diagnosis of a terminal illness, usually measured by a prognosis of six months or less left to live."[7] There is flexibility on the time frame to be sure. Some hospice services will extend the length of time up to a year or even take a more flexible approach that doesn't specify any length of time at all. Policies then are broadened in a way to suggest that the patient has a limited life expectancy or is at an end-stage of a life-threatening illness or disease that cannot be cured.

Second is that a patient "is seeking comfort-oriented care, rather than treatment aimed at cure . . . Some hospices may have a list of medical treatments that are considered 'hospice-appropriate' or else [medicines and treatments] that are excluded from hospice coverage. Treatments to relieve the patient's pain – no matter how expensive or high-tech – are typically included in a hospice program."[8]

A *third* requirement is that, the "patient and family are informed about hospice and other options and consent in writing to hospice care; the patient's physician also consents to hospice."[9] In short, people have to understand what they are getting into. They cannot have incorrect notions about the purpose of hospice care. "With any medical treatment there is the danger of miscommunication between provider and patient, inadequate exchange of information, or unmet expectations. With hospice care the danger is more serious, because hospice proposes to make the dying patient comfortable, [and] not to provide a medical cure. If that is not what the patient and family want, then serious disappointments or conflicts may follow. Often the hospice admission process explicitly states or implies that the patient should want to be *maintained at home* for as long as possible and that the family is willing and able to participate in the patient's care at home."[10]

"Hospice cannot admit a patient if the physician is opposed, so it is necessary to discuss the hospice option with the physician and find out why he or she may be opposed. If the patient is seeking a program of care for the dying, and the doctor doesn't believe the patient is terminally ill, obviously there is a misunderstanding somewhere."[11]

A *fourth* requirement is that hospice must be provided in a safe setting for care. "This requirement is defined in different ways by different hospices, but with the overall goal that hospice care is attempted under circumstances that are realistic and workable – such as a secure home environment with safe arrangements for hospice staff to visit the home and, usually, the presence of the family caregiver."[12] If someone lives alone and is at the end-stage of life, there will come a time when she is no longer able to care for herself. Because this is a reality for every end-of-life patient, hospices reluctantly turn away those who do not have someone who can help them. Some hospice services are experimenting with ways to serve those who have no family by enlisting friends, neighbors, church members and others who can give the help that is needed.

A *fifth* requirement is that there is a "do not resuscitate (DNR) order posted near the patient, meaning that the patient – and the patient's doctor – agree in advance that no cardiopulmonary resuscitation (CPR) or other heroic measures will be attempted if the patient's heart stopped beating."[13] Such heroic measures do not promote life but merely delay death. Grace and I were required to post a DNR document in the window of the back door of our home so that anyone entering would be aware of the situation.

There may be other requirements or limitations to using hospice care such as geographical service boundaries. Hospice nurses and staff of other supporting services must be able to travel in some cases rather quickly to a home hospice setting.

Grace was on Medicare throughout her last illness and that fact made our choice for hospice a little easier. There were absolutely no costs to us whatsoever, and nothing was denied to her for her palliative care. When she was still able to stand and take a few steps only, a walker was approved; when she required a wheelchair, it was provided. At one point the hospice nurse was concerned about Grace's difficulty in breathing and oxygen was prescribed. When Grace needed a bathing chair, it was supplied and when the time came that she needed an adjustable hospital bed, it was delivered and set up. Required prescriptions, including pain-numbing opiates, were delivered to our front door usually on the day they were prescribed. All of this and more was provided without charge to us.

My wife wished to die at home. She realized her wish, but I cannot imagine how I would have coped with her painful decline and death by myself. I am grateful for the patient counsel of the staff as they answered my questions about the signs and stages of advancing death; as they showed me how to remove needles, clean and dress the area of my wife's port after infusions; as they explained the use of the various drugs that made Grace's final days much more comfortable than they would have been without them; as they taught me techniques for bathing and changing my wife when she became completely bedridden. They made sure that I could reposition my wife to change her positions and to enable me to change the bedding while she was on the bed.

Since the primary reason we were created is to give glory to God, I have to believe that even under those adverse circumstances, God would be glorified, acknowledged as righteous, loving, and doing good. It was a difficult test of faith to take this view as I watched my wife's suffering – and tried to share in that suffering – but it is what God's word calls us to do. God gives us the strength and the grace to do what he calls us to do.

If you and your wife know that she is near the end of her life, and she wishes to die at home, do look into hospice services. There are probably several in your greater community from which you could choose. You still have time to investigate your options, and I would urge you to do so. No dying is easy, but a hospice will help to make less difficult.

<u>DURING</u>

Chapter Six

Final Arrangements

"Precious in the sight of the LORD is the death of his saints. (Psalm 116:15)

The Reality Of Death

On the twenty-third of the month of March, early in the morning, Grace was with me. We spoke. I helped her reposition herself. A little while later she lay motionless; she was not with me anymore. My love was still there but the loving living relationship that spanned forty-seven years had come to an end. I was shaken. I simply sat and watched her lifeless body, wondering if she would move or do anything to indicate that she was still alive. I knew that the time had come. There was no urgent call for medical assistance. I sat in silence almost as motionless as she. I prayed a simple prayer: "King of souls, welcome her into your presence today," with a sense of peace and relief knowing that my wife would suffer no more, and that her spirit was with God.

Seeing her without spirit, I was reminded of a psalm of which I have become particularly fond. Psalm 104 speaks of the might, the mystery and the majesty of God. One of the statements of that psalm seemed timely: "When you hide your face, they are dismayed; when you take away their breath, they die and return to their dust."[1] God sustains all life – your life as you read this – and, "if he should recall his spirit and his breath, all flesh would perish together and man would return to dust.[2]" Speaking of those who have died, the psalmist's words mirror sentiments of Job: "When his breath departs he returns to the earth; on that very day his plans perish.[3]" Seeing my wife in her stillness also reminded me of my own mortality. One day I will lie as still as she. This is the destiny of all humanity but there is another glorious reality for those who through faith have eternal life in Christ Jesus: their "dust" will rise at the last day glorious, beautiful, perfect and fully alive in every way possible, a state that will continue forever (See chapter eight below). These comforting thoughts entered my mind as well.

I wondered what specifically the spirit of my wife was doing. Could she see me sitting in my chair as she was escorted into the presence of Christ? Had all thoughts of her life faded by the overwhelming glories of heaven? I knew that all her suffering had come to an end, but what was she experiencing at the very moment of death? I wondered just how I would relate to her when my turn to die would come. I know that our earthly relationship had come to an end, but what would it be later? There are those who are unnecessarily troubled by these thoughts. The Bible is not as clear on what that relationship will be as it is on what that relationship will not be. Christ provided straightforward teaching on the subject.

Heaven and Marriage

"Will I see my wife again; will I know my wife in heaven?" Christians are told as a matter of doctrinal instruction that death is the temporary separation of body and soul, which separation will be resolved at the resurrection and in the final state. Everyone who believes in God must from time to time think about what happens to the soul at death and what the afterlife is going to be like. Well, the answer to both of those first two questions is, "Yes". If you and your wife shared faith in Christ, then you will see and know your wife in heaven. There is nothing in Scripture that would indicate otherwise! You will see and know the Savior. You will see his glorified body and the wounds in his body that he received in procuring your salvation. If all believers will see and know him, there is no reason to doubt that we will see and know others whom we have loved, and we will love others whom we have not known.

A deeper question behind such concerns has to do with the nature of the relationship between a believing husband and a believing wife. Christians will not be married in heaven! Nothing could be clearer than Jesus' answer to questions put to him by the Sadducees about this very matter. The Sadducees did not believe in angels or spirits; they did not believe in the afterlife, and they did not believe in the resurrection.[4] They approached Jesus with a "what-if" situation based upon the requirements of the Old Testament law that if a married man died without fathering an heir to carry on his name, his brother would be required to take his dead brother's wife and attempt to father an heir for his brother.[5] The Sadducees posed a hypothetical situation for Jesus in which seven men who were brothers married the same widow and failed in their attempts to father an heir for their brother who had initially married the woman. They questioned Jesus about whose wife the woman would be in the resurrection since all seven had her as a wife. Jesus said that the Sadducees were wrong on two accounts: first of all, they did not understand the Scriptures, and they did not believe in the power of God (to raise the dead). Jesus affirmed the afterlife and the resurrection, which the Sadducees repudiated. He also stated that in the resurrection, "They neither marry nor are [they] given in marriage."[6] According to Scripture, the marriage bond is severed when one of the partners in the marriage dies.[7] Believers do not remarry in heaven nor are marriages contracted in heaven. So, the Sadducees were wrong on the second count. Then Jesus went on to say that they (that is the resurrected saints) are like the angels in heaven.[8] He was not suggesting that they will be genderless, but that there will not be marriage in heaven because there will be no need for it. Marriage is an earthbound institution and governed largely by time. The Word of God makes very clear that there are specific purposes for marriage in this age.

Many marriage ceremonies begin with words having to do with the reason people are gathered on that specific occasion. It is to join a man and woman together in holy marriage. Shortly after that statement there is often another having to do with marriage being a divine institution, instituted by God himself in the Garden of Eden.[9] Twice in that account, the woman is referred to as Adam's wife. Also, it is clear that marriage calls for the proper leaving the one's parents in order to establish a new home and family.[10] Divorce was permitted in the Law of Moses, but Jesus cited a creation ordinance: "From the beginning... he who created them made them male and female and said, 'Therefore, a man shall leave his father and his mother and hold fast to his wife . . . '"[11]

The word of God has provided several reasons for marriage, one of which was mentioned in the passage cited above. God made woman and brought her to the man, because there was no suitable helper for the man. Marriage is a union in which a man and woman are unified in the work that they do; they give and receive help mutually. Initially stated, the woman was given to the man so he would have a helper. The New Testament is clear on the helping, supporting role of the man with his wife. The love a man should have for his wife is seen by his caring for, providing for and nourishing his wife.[12] The apostle Peter wrote about the husband giving proper honor to his wife.[13] Neither husband nor wife could carry out all their responsibilities as they should under the authority of the parents of either of them. God wisely ordained that a husband and wife establish a particular and distinct household. The advantages to this divine arrangement are multiple.

What's more, a secure home is the setting for having children. It is the context in which God ordained for them to be born and reared. God directed the first couple to be fruitful and to multiply. He did this before the entrance of sin into the world.[14] He restated his directive after the flood.[15] A trial marriage or no marriage at all is a commitment-less environment that promotes insecurity and instability in children. The prophet Malachi reminded God's people that they should be faithful in keeping their marriage vows. Such covenant keeping fosters the environment for having children – "a godly seed" to use Malachi's words.[16] Having children within a family context is what God intended from the beginning. Husbands and wives come together as one flesh and produce children by that union.

Marriage is also for the mutual sanctification of those couples who give themselves freely to one another. In such a marriage husband and wife help to keep each other from falling into lusts or sexual sins.[17] It is also for the mutual pleasure of one another.[18] What is more, living together in the bond of marriage as God intended, tends to promote godliness.[19] As husband and wife put on the full armor of God,[20] together they engage in spiritual warfare and they may assist each other in that struggle. The closest human relationship is between husband and wife. A husband and wife mutually serve as each other's friend, confidant, helper and lover.

In the final state, after the resurrection, there will no longer be death. There will not be a need for procreation. The population of heaven will not be diminished by death. In that respect, we will be like the angels. Angels do not die and there has never been a need to produce more of them.

In heaven we will not need the kind of marital help to survive as we do on this side of heaven; we will be perfect in holiness, the sanctification process will have ended; there will be no spiritual enemy and no spiritual warfare for which we would need to put on spiritual armor; there will not be a need to procreate. All the reasons for marriage in this life will no longer exist, and the saints will have perfect communion with each other and the Lord. As wonderful as the state of marriage is, there will be no need for it in the perfect state. Those saved ones who have been married in this life will see and know one another in heaven, but their relationship will not be the same as it was on earth.

Attending To The Immediate

My wife had been in hospice care in our home, so I was with her until the very end of her physical life. She died at 5:20 am. I called for the hospice nurse who said she would come right away, but due to a late season snowstorm, what ordinarily was a twenty-minute trip took three hours. Shortly after the hospice nurse arrived she pronounced my wife dead and called the funeral home. I had made arrangements anticipating this day and the need. The funeral director and his assistant came within a half hour, expressed their condolences, and took my wife away. They asked that I not be present during the preparing of her body for removal. I went downstairs and waited for them to take her out of our home. After a few moments of consoling me, the hospice care nurse left too.

The house seemed eerily quiet. I walked through the rooms slowly several times. All the equipment associated with her care – the hospital bed, oxygen, the IV stand and tubes, wheelchair, bathing chair, the table with the medications – were there as silent witnesses to what my wife had endured. I could not have them in the house; could not have them there. Late morning on the twenty-third, I began to dismantle the bed and move all the equipment to the back door where it could be taken away as quickly as possible. I called the hospice supply people to come and retrieve their equipment. In early afternoon all of it was gone.

I called my children to let them know that their mom had passed on. They knew that that call would come. They were as ready as they could be for that moment. I had arranged a phone tree that would save me making several calls that morning. There were just four calls I needed to make besides calling my three children. Each of those persons called were asked to notify other individuals and to give them the basic information of what had transpired that morning. The specifics of the services could not be provided since they were pending. The call tree saved me making multiple calls to repeat the same information. It took away some of the immediacy of activity in which others could share. I notified the minister and the elders of the church to let them know as well. All of them were genuinely sorrowful and gracious in their expressions of condolence. All offered any help they could give. The church family was apprised and on the Sunday following my wife's passing, her home-going was announced publically. Other members of both sides of the family were notified, as were several friends.

Chapter Seven

Meeting With The Funeralist

All things should be done decently and in order. (1 Corinthians 14:10)

If you anticipate the passing of your wife, it would be well that you make a list of the things that will need to be done at the time of her death. This may sound cold or insensitive, but it is the reality you will face. Some decisions cannot be made until her death occurs. At that time they will need to be made promptly and you may not be in an emotional state to make them well. You do not have to wait until your wife's death however, to make certain decisions.

Part of wisdom is knowing *that* you need help. Immediately following the death of your wife is one of those times when you will need help. Several things will press upon you when your wife dies – whether her death was long-anticipated or not. I expect that you know this is true. Understanding that you will require help leads you to ask the question of what *kind* of help you will need. Get some advice to determine *what* things need to be done and *when* they need to be done. Consulting with the funeralist will clarify some of decisions you will have to make.

Part of wisdom is knowing *when* you need help, and *further*, part of wisdom is knowing that it would be better for you in your situation to allow others who have more time and more energy than you do, more specific knowledge of a subject than you do, more skill in specific disciplines than you do, to help you and even to do certain tasks *for* you! If your experience will be anything like mine, you will discover just how willing and appreciative those are whom you will ask for help! That should be the sequence: What, when and who. Find others to help do what you could very well do yourself, but what you do not need personally to do.

Once you are settled on what has to be done, enlist others to help you. There are some things that are personal, private, and require choices that you alone must make. You have to attend to those yourself, but at the same time, determine those things that others could do just as well as you, and perhaps even better than you. You personally do not have to do them. Decide what you and you alone must do.

Next, decide whom you will ask to do those things for you. Do you have a good friend whom you can trust to do a personal errand, to make a decision, or to assume a particular responsibility? Could a family member take responsibility for various "must-do's". Choose someone(s) whom you can trust to do the specific "Whats".

Since my wife's decline was gradual, I had the advantage of planning a funeral in detail, but I knew also that several telephone calls would have to be made after my wife had actually passed away. I had identified four persons who would serve as disseminators of information. Those persons were to call several other people – friends, family members on both sides, work associates, etc. – to tell them what had taken place and to let them know about visitation and funeral services. It was a significant relief knowing that after only four brief phone conversations scores of people would know about the particulars of Grace's passing and of the arrangements that were to be made.

People will want to help you as they helped me. When my wife passed away, someone volunteered to have a bulletin prepared, which would be distributed at the time of my wife's funeral. I was glad he took on the task; I didn't have to think about it a second time. On the matter of what my wife would wear for her final appearance, my daughter made the decision, to which I simply gave the nod. Someone else asked the women in the church to arrange after-service refreshments. They did a superb job. I didn't need to concern myself with that matter in the least. Someone offered to produce a map with directions from the funeral home to the church where the funeral service would take place. I was grateful for something as simple as that; I didn't need to think about how the many friends and relatives coming from out of town would find their way to the church building a few miles away from the funeral home. I forwarded several pictures of my wife to an individual who put them together in a scrolling presentation that would run on a digital media frame during the visitation. He assumed the responsibility and produced a disk to be used at that time. I didn't have to think about the matter any further.

Initial Matters

I had had an initial conversation with a funeral director prior to my wife's death. Matters of taking her from my home to the funeral home had been arranged well in advance of her passing. The funeral director had been apprised of the hospice situation and knew that he could expect a call from me. When the funeral home staff came to remove my wife, I scheduled a meeting for the next day when more specific details of her funeral could be addressed. Various options regarding the service, including the kind of coffin, music if any to be played during the visitation, burial permit, death certificate(s), public notification, flower arrangements and more were discussed and decided at that meeting. Usually, there is a format followed by the funeralist's staff to make sure all these matters are covered in a systematic way. A line item amount for each part of the professional services made it easier to track the total costs of the funeral. It is well to anticipate these final costs and to set funds aside for them.

My daughter arrived within a couple of days of her mother's passing to help arrange all the other matters related to the funeral. We went to a local floral shop and selected various flower arrangements. The funeral director had lent me three large bulletin boards that could be used for posting pictures. My daughter and I went through the family picture albums and selected a representative sampling of my wife's youth; the early days of our marriage; and more recent times. We placed them on the three bulletin boards and had the boards positioned in the visitation room.

We also completed the clothing options for my wife's last appearance, making sure to include accessories that reflected her national roots. My wife had made a few suggestions about her clothing during the last couple of weeks of her life. We had discussed that matter together freely. We discussed the possibility of a closed casket, which my wife preferred since she had declined remarkably during her illness, but said she would not insist upon it. She agreed that I and the children should make that decision. In fact, the children and I chose to have an open casket at the visitation. Grace was concerned about how she would look the last time people would see her. It is almost humorous now, but when she and I had the conversation about open or closed casket, she was concerned that she wouldn't have anything to wear. She *had* lost significant weight. The casket was closed during the funeral service (See chapter eight below.).

The visitation and funeral would be exactly one week after my wife died. That length of time between the two events seemed sufficient to allow people who wished to attend to alter their schedules. Even though I had known of the imminent death of my wife, there still were several matters I had to deal with immediately following her death. I had to decide on the particulars of the funeral: the kind of funeral I wanted, when I wanted visitation to begin and when I wanted it to end; and certainly, the costs were discussed and decisions made in a relatively short time.

Grace's interment would be out of state, so to conclude visitation at the funeral home, I chose to have a committal service prior to the funeral service at the church. I asked our associate pastor to bring the words of comfort and counsel at that time in lieu of a graveside service.

If you have assumed the responsibility for planning your wife's funeral service, be assured that forms for these services are readily available. For your help, there are funeral planners that have checklists to assist you in making your decisions about what you may want to include. A sample checklist appears in Appendix B. You can use these forms or simply employ them to formulate your own ideas about the service. Those of you who may be asked to assist someone in making these decisions at this time of loss, may use these forms to help you talk through these delicate matters with him.

Costs

Be prepared for the cost of the funeral. As everything else, the price of laying a loved one to rest continues to rise as does everything else. Since funeral services provided by funeral directors are not purchased frequently, those who need them are often shocked by the expense. Latest Federal Trade Commission estimates for funeral costs range from $8,000 and upward – the average at about $10,000.[1] Some of these costs are identified in Appendix C. The price of a coffin alone may run from $2,500 to several thousand dollars higher depending upon the materials from which the coffin is made, and the amount of ornate styling it features, and so forth. The burial plot and interment may push $4,000 considering the grave site, grave opening and closing, grave marker and/or head stone. Again, the cost of the headstone ranges widely. Its cost may approach the cost of the basic services provided by a funeral director. Providers of funerals offer pre-paid services, which essentially lock in costs. Some who are anticipating the death of a loved one have taken advantage of these services. Others have opted to anticipate these costs through funeral insurance. If the death of your wife is a matter of a relatively short time away, it would be well to make yourself aware of the current cost of the funeral in your area. Those of you who wish to minister to someone who is grieving the loss of his wife, may also find it helpful in your conversations with him to be aware of his financial outlay. You might also accompany your friend on his conference(s) with a funeral director. Someone has said that life's hardest decisions come at life's hardest times. At one of the most difficult times of grieving, your friend will be asked to make decisions that he may not be prepared easily to make. Your support, your thoughts and opinions might help to make his grieving less traumatic.

Chapter Eight

Visitation And Funeral

The Lord has given and the Lord has taken away. Blessed is the name of the Lord. (Job 1:21)

Funerals In The Biblical Record

When Job received the devastating news of the death of all his children, not to mention the loss of his possessions, he responded with worship. The Bible does not provide any information about what kind of funeral Job gave for his sons and daughters. It tells, however, about Job's heart and that he expressed his sorrow in the worship of the LORD.

We have only limited information about the funeral practices of God's people in the Old Testament period. The earliest account is that of Abraham burying his wife Sarah. Nothing is mentioned about a ritual, but simply that Abraham mourned for his wife and that he wept for her.[1] Abraham's sorrow was obvious; his tears flowed freely. Readers learn that he did not have a burial site and needed to acquire one quickly in order to bury, "my dead out of my sight."[2] The greater context suggests that Abraham intended that the plot of land he had purchased to be used for multiple burials. That plot became Abraham's resting place as well.[3] When Esau and Jacob buried their father Isaac, it was in the same field where Isaac's parents were buried.[4] Jacob buried his favorite wife Rachel away from the family plot, but he erected a monument to mark the site of the burial. He did bury Leah with the patriarchal family at Machpelah.[5] Jacob was told that his son Joseph would "close his eyes".[6] Joseph was present at the death of his father and showed his grief by weeping over his father and by kissing him. He attended to the details of his father's interment, including the embalming of Jacob's body, and when that process was completed, he received permission to leave Egypt and to bury his father where the rest of the covenant family had been entombed. Again, there was a very great and grievous lament and an additional seven days of mourning.

When Joseph died, he was embalmed, and years later when the Israelites left Egypt and settled in Canaan, he was buried on his inherited land in Ephraim, which had been given to him by his father Jacob.[7]

It was probably the custom to have family burial sites where several generations would be laid to rest. Joshua was buried on his inherited land;[8] Samuel was interred at his house in Ramah;[9] Joab was entombed at his home in the wilderness;[10] King Manasseh in the garden at his home;[11] King Josiah was laid to rest in the same tomb as his father and grandfather,[12] a site that was probably used by his family for generations.[13] Since land was not to be sold permanently, but remain in the family, it would seem that each family would designate an area as a cemetery.

"When we examine those funeral arrangements that were made and recounted in the Gospels at the time of the death of our Lord, we get a glimpse of what must have been a standard practice at the time. The body was treated with respect and placed in a special spot reserved to receive the bodies of the dead. Those who were close to the dead person in life continued their closeness through the ministrations made in death. This included the . . . preparation of the body for entombment and the ceremonial events. Various members of the family and circle of close friends made their visits to the sepulcher to fulfill their own sense of obligation, realizing the necessity to fulfill these obligations to the best of their ability."[14]

The dead were treated lovingly. Friends and family members would wash the body[15] and use aromatic spices to prepare it for burial. Hands and feet were tied, and then a tunic was used to wrap the body. The mouth was closed and covered with a separate cloth.[16] It appears that besides the use of spices, fragrant perfumes or ointments served to mask the odor of decay,[17] and the dead, being prepared in this way would be placed on a bed or couch prior to their burial as in the case of Dorcas [Tabitha] and Jairus' daughter.[18] The bodies would be wrapped in a tunic, placed on a stretcher-like bier and carried to the place of burial. "Mourners" would lead the procession, followed by the family and friends. It was relatively easy for Jesus to approach the bier of the son of the widow at Nain.[19]

Embalming was not practiced by the Israelites, but due to the direction of Joseph, Jacob was embalmed and so was Joseph, who was second only to the Pharaoh in Egypt. Ordinarily, burial of the dead was done quickly because of rapid decomposition in that part of the world, and the desire to avoid defilement through contact with the dead. "[This] in part explains the quickness with which the bodies of Nadab and Abihu were carried out of the [Israelite] camp [Leviticus 10], and those of Ananias and Sapphira were hastened to burial."[20] "The dead [were] often in their graves, according to . . . custom, within two or three hours after death."[21]

Death and Culture

People of all cultures have developed traditions on how they deal with the death of family members. "Mourning is learned. Mourning moves us through grief. It is the outward expression of grief – any action that helps us adapt to our loss. Mourning is influenced primarily by the culture in which we grew up, and secondarily by the culture in which we live as adults."[22] Societies practice rituals that seek to honor the dead, to equip them for an afterlife, and to comfort those closest to the deceased. The belief systems of those cultures and societies inform those rituals. Symbols and ceremonies convey beliefs about what has happened to the deceased and what, it is believed, lies ahead for the spirit of the departed. "[E]very group in every culture has found it necessary to perform certain rituals at the time of the death of its members."[23]

Modern Western culture is no different. Beliefs about the destiny of the dead have been incorporated into funeral practices. Rituals remind mourners of what the deceased may expect and what, it is hoped, they are experiencing. Various religious traditions have developed orders of service for funerals as well. Components of such services might include a recognition of the life and contributions (legacy) of the deceased, words of testimony, music, a statement concerning the beliefs about death and a future life, consoling and comforting the grieving family, wider instruction for all who are present. Words of instruction and invocation are spoken; words of comfort and hope are expressed. Belief about the place of the life lived and about the future existence of the deceased are reviewed and reinforced. Words of comfort are conveyed, various religious traditions have developed the orders of service for funerals.

First Funerals

I was about six years old when my grandpa took me to visit my great-grandmother in a nursing home. Before her relocation to that nursing home, she had lived two doors away from my maternal grandparents. Occasionally, I would go to visit her there. She would give me a glass of milk and a cookie. Great-grandma's health deteriorated and nursing home care became necessary. One day my grandpa asked if I would like to go with him to visit his mother. I said, "Yes". During that visit I distinctly remember a disagreement between my grandpa and his mother. She felt as though life was over for her; she wanted to die and to go to heaven. My grandpa didn't like the idea. He thought his mother should make the most of life as long as the Lord extended it. He believed there is always a service that those who live perform for the Lord. The disagreement continued as I sat in six-year-old silence among much older adults. A couple of weeks later, great-grandma died in her room; the Lord had granted her wish.

The funeral was "old world," a lot of formalities, pleasantries, and whispers during the visitation. I understood I would not see the great grandma who had given me the cookies and milk again.

Later that summer, I attended my second funeral. My best friend in first grade was hit and killed by a car. At the visitation, I overheard his father tell my father: "The last thing I said to him was, 'Be careful when you cross the street.' He said, 'Okay dad,' ran out the front door and was struck by a car." I saw the grief on the face of my friend's father.

There were other funerals: my maternal grandmother died when I was 13, and an uncle a short time later, but the greatest force of the reality of death came when a younger brother was killed in Viet Nam. Until that time, I had taken the reports of the mounting death tolls during that conflict as a matter of statistics. I had been married less than a year. My parents were shaken to the core. The word seems overly used, but my brother's death *devastated* them.

My mother cried and sobbed until she ran out of tears; my dad just went silent. Nothing like that ever had happened in our extended family. My dad had lived through the carnage of World War II and his dad had been in World War I. Uncles had served during the Korean conflict, but this was a crushing experience for the entire, extended family. I still vividly remember the funeral and the graveside service. As long as I live I will remember that service. My grandparents went in their turn, as did my parents, living out their days. Their funeral services were somber reminders that death comes to everyone. There is sorrow, sadness, and numbness. Words cannot adequately describe the feelings. Then one of my granddaughters died at birth, not living one day. The deaths of people older than I seemed to mark the passing of the generations. Not so in this case. The sorrow for my son and daughter-in-law was profound; they experienced a deep sense of loss even though their daughter had not lived into her second day. There is that time to be born and a time to die.[24] King Solomon taught, "It is better to go to the house of mourning than to go to the house of feasting, for this is the end of all mankind. The living (should) take it to heart."[25]

The brother and servant of the Lord wrote this in his letter to the church: "Come now, you who say, 'Today or tomorrow we will go into such and such a town and spend a year there and trade and make a profit' – yet you do not know what tomorrow will bring. What is your life; for you are a mist that appears for a little time and then vanishes? Instead you ought to say, 'If the Lord wills, we will live and do this or that.'"[26] A friend of mine regularly reminds people of the uncertainty of life and the certainty of death with the words of Ecclesiastes 9:12: "Man knows not this time." Those words should provoke thoughts about the end of life. A question of an earlier generation is not frequently asked in this one: "Are you ready to meet God?" We do not have a guarantee of our next breath or heartbeat. The aged, middle-aged, youth, and newborn face the same prospect, that of the uncertain timing of certain death. God has given us his word so that those who believed in him may know how to glorify and enjoy God in this lifetime. As no other volume can, that same word of God prepares us for death, and our great appointment to stand before God. Are you ready to meet God? There is no more appropriate time to consider your answer to that question than in the face of the approaching death of a loved one.

But, why death at all? Death, rather than being the way of nature, is not natural. It was not part of God's original order. It is not part of a natural cycle to which we must stoically become adjusted. All cultures and all religions have their explanations. Some deny that a death has taken place! The Bible's explanation is clear. The opening chapters of Genesis link death to defection and disobedience. God created the man and the woman, placed them in a pristine setting, gave them various responsibilities and a command, the breaking of which would bring about their deaths. Believing this account might seem naïve to you, but its truth is assumed by the rest of the entire Bible – both Old and New Testaments.

When our first parents sinned against God by violating the command he had given them, they experienced the death he had threatened. "In the day you eat [of the fruit of the Tree of the Knowledge of Good and Evil] you shall surely die."[27] Adam's and Eve's bodies did not collapse into dust at that moment, but spiritually their favorable relationship to God ended; and, if God had not intervened, they would have certainly died eternally. Their bodies became infected with corruption and deteriorated so that eventually, the sentence that God had threatened was carried out. God said to them: "You are dust and to dust you shall return."[28] Everyone shares in the corruption of our first parents; everyone inherits the guilt of sin and everyone dies.[29] The word of God clearly attaches a spiritual significance to physical death;[30] "the wages of sin is death."[31]

The vast majority of people avoid this connection, but little is clearer in the word of God.[32]

All people are spiritually dead due to the sin of Adam,[33] and unless they are reborn, they will remain under God's judgment[34] and will experience eternal death.

New and eternal life resided within the apostle Paul, but his body had an appointment with death. Paul exclaimed: "Wretched man that I am. Who will deliver me from this body of death?"[35] His body was and everyone's body is characterized by death and is destined for death.

Rather than to acknowledge this connection and take steps to avert the ultimate consequences of sin, humanity has denied death or defied death. Edgar Jackson speaks of modern man living "more and more in a death-denying, death-defying state."[36] People speak popularly of death not as the end of natural life, but of existing on another plane, or of being part of a natural cycle, which we should embrace rather than resisted. Death is reevaluated, redefined and thought of in philosophical or metaphysical terms. Death is viewed as essentially a medical challenge with no reference to its spiritual dynamic.

We live in a day when members of our affluent western society have enjoyed the enhancements to and the prolongation of life through living healthier lifestyles and advances in medical technology, which have increased life expectancy. Modern medicine has virtually eliminated, or has been able successfully to treat what in earlier times were life-ending diseases. The hope for the future is that research will be able to customize medications to each unique individual, virtually tailor-making medicines. Implicit in this hope is the belief that medical science will eventually cure death. Of course, this view is unrealistic. Everyone eventually dies. Yet, there remains in the collective mind the thought that death can be delayed; that it doesn't have to be faced at the moment, any serious discussion about its inevitability may be postponed or avoided altogether. Consequently, a funeral marks a failure in technology and signals that so much more work needs to be done.

Others view funerals as a sociological phenomenon. Robert Fulton identified three purposes of funeral rites: 1) properly to dispose of a dead body; 2) to aid the bereaved to reorient themselves from the shock of death; and, 3) to acknowledge publicly and commemorate a death while asserting the viability of the *group* [italics mine].[37] A funeral is thought of as a rite of passage, but also something that reaffirms the social character of human existence. It is a "form of group protection, in the face of individual death, to affirm the values of life and the community, and direct future living toward these values."[38] It functions to reserve the freedoms of the future by offering occasion to let go of the past. This sociological perspective of funerals stresses the protection of the grievers;

it is considered a group-centered response to death. Death is regarded as something that happens to the group.

What's more, at one time funerals were viewed as psychological releases. They were perceived as "efforts of individuals to build defenses against the painful or unpleasant[ness]" of life.[39] Consequently, a funeral was regarded by some psychologists as part of the process of "freeing one's self from bondage to the deceased."[40] It was thought to provide a climate for doing what sooner or later [psychologically] has to be done.

These approaches tend to depersonalize death. If your grief associated with death can be explained in terms of these disciplines, then you are well on your way to denying your personal grief; and, if you can deny your own grief, you will diminish the grief that others are experiencing. You will decrease your sensitivity to the pain of others, perhaps even suggesting that their sorrow is light and passing, that they'll "get over it," or that they should do a better job at controlling their emotions.

The Services

Grace's visitation and funeral were on the thirtieth of the month, and frankly, the particulars of that day are a blur. I see faces floating before my consciousness. I remember that many warm, consoling and gracious words were spoken, but I don't remember anything anyone actually said. Saying that may sound terribly insensitive, but it is true! I have a good idea of who came to express sympathies – including some neighbors whose interaction with Grace and me previously had been little more than a friendly wave and a mutual nodding of the head. People I had not seen in years came to the visitation. They wanted to pay their respects and they did. Some family members traveled significant distances to be present. I won't forget that.

At the funeral service later, the church building was filled. I've attended funerals that relatively few people attended, but it was not the case with my wife's funeral. That the meeting area was filled was a tribute to my wife and to the affection that those present had for her.

The minister gave a very appropriate and comforting message based on Psalm 90:1-7. His words were as much for the benefit of everyone present as they were for me and the immediate family. After the service there was the standard greeting and refreshments in the church fellowship hall. I had had a cup of coffee in the morning of the funeral, but did not feel like eating a thing for breakfast. While the guests mingled and munched, I was greeting people; the greeting line seemed endless. Finally, around 4:30 after nearly everyone had left, I got a bite to eat.

Purpose

At this point, I want to return to the matter of the purpose of a funeral. Some do think of a funeral from a medical or sociological or psychological perspective – but most assuredly, not those experiencing the loss of the deceased. Some see a funeral as a way of saying "goodbye". I expect that funerals are simply that for many people. After all, in this life we will no longer see or interact with the deceased person. It is a "goodbye" in which only one side participates and in that sense a funeral is for the benefit of the living. Yet, let us consider the bigger picture. There is a well-known catechism that asks as its first question: "What is man's primary purpose?" The answer it gives is: "Man's primary purpose is to glorify God and to enjoy him forever."[41] The grace of God and the truth of the gospel should be evident in our lives by how we respond to suffering and hardships. When we respond to them graciously, we bring glory to God. This is no less true for those who experience the loss of a loved one. What we believe about life and death is seen at a funeral. Are we merely depositing a body in the soil of earth or are we formally sending off a soul to heaven? Are we merely saying "Farewell" or "Goodbye"? Routinely, funeral services have these components or some variation of them.

- Commemoration: The deceased is remembered for the life lived and the legacy left.

- Confession: The faith of the deceased concerning life, death and the afterlife is declared.

- Commentary: Those gathered are instructed, exhorted, and encouraged from the Scriptures.

- Consolation: The words of Scripture's comfort are spoken.

- Canticles: The singing expresses the hope and faith of the community of faith.

- Confidence: The promises of God about his peace and continued faithfulness are repeated

- Committal: The burial occasions assurance of the resurrection and everlasting life.

Since the Bible makes clear that people are to give glory to God in all things and under every circumstance,[42] we must show what we believe by what we do and what we do not do at the time of the funeral. How can we give glory to God at a funeral? For starters, we can acknowledge that God is the source and the sustainer of life; he brings it about, continues it as long as he sees fit, and brings it to an end in his good time. It is God's divine prerogative to shorten or extend life.[43]

During a funeral there is also the opportunity to thank and praise God for the grace demonstrated in the life and in the death of the departed loved one, who through some extremely difficult circumstances, lived his/her life to the glory of God. If you were able to ask the late believer how she did it; if you were to ask how she was able to endure, you would hear testimony to the grace of God. She may have suffered severely without complaints to God or to anyone else, yet would testify to God's grace at work in her to the praise of God's glory.

She may have lived a life characterized by good deeds, which deeds were performed by God's grace. Those works were performed out of gratitude for God's gracious gifts, the greatest of which is eternal life through Jesus Christ. A mild and contented life, with rarely a harsh or critical word to others, and a bearing up under inordinate difficulties would testify to the grace of God operative in that person's life to the praise of God's glory. That person may have died without any doubts about God's goodness and without any questions about God's sovereignty in bringing her through her last illness. She may have suffered with all the rest of humanity, but not as all the rest of humanity suffers. She had suffered with faith in the God of grace to the praise of his glory. These things and others should be brought out at a Christian's funeral. Similarly, the manner in which believing mourners mourn *should be* reflected in the funeralizing of a believer who has passed.

Another purpose of a funeral is to provide occasion to remind everyone in attendance of the brevity of life and the certainty of death. The book of the Psalms states: "The years of our life are seventy, or even by reason of strength eighty; yet their span is but toil and trouble; they are soon gone, and we fly away;"[44] and the New Testament declares: "You do not know what tomorrow will bring. What is your life? For you are a mist that appears for a little time and then vanishes."[45] All present *should be* keenly interested in this reminder. All present will eventually be in the same state as one who is funeralized. All might not be in the same blessed state, but each one will absolutely face death. Why would they not want to prepare for the inevitable? The one who addresses those gathered has the privilege of reminding everyone of the certainty of death, which death is followed by giving an account of one's life to God.[46] Some people who will attend would never darken the doors of a church. The Christian's funeral should serve as a testimony to the grace of the God of both the living and the dead.

Then too, consider the matters of consolation and communion. Gathered at a funeral will be people of faith and people without saving faith. There is opportunity for the speaker to console believers and nonbelievers alike from the word of God. Let God's people be unified in the comfort they received publicly from God's word. Let those who are not believers witness the consolation and promise that God gives to his people. The words of Scripture bring comfort like no other spoken word. Let the people of God be unified in their communion, encouraging and comforting one another in the context of the community of faith. What a powerful witness to believers and non-believers alike! Such may take place; such should take place at a Christian's funeral.

In the Protestant tradition, the funeral service is most often led by a minister of the congregation to which the deceased had belonged. A selection of Scripture appropriate for the occasion is read, and then explained and applied. Those scriptures should be part of the basis for the faith confessed by the community of faith to which the deceased belonged. The faith confessed is faith in the One who died and lives forever. He faced death and overcame its power; he removed the cause of death. He, in his real and representative death, experienced the eternal death that awaits those who do not have saving faith in him. Christ lived the perfect life to make his people righteous; he died the perfect death to pay for their offenses against God. The benefits of Christ's life and death come to those who are united to him through saving faith.

Christ arose from death and by that resurrection, God showed his acceptance of Christ's death on behalf of all who have faith in him. One of those benefits is the spiritual strength to live in this age which *is* characterized by misery and death, but another is enjoying the hope of continued eternal life after the close of this age, which is not interrupted by death. How can it be otherwise when we read words like this from the one who conquered death? "I am the resurrection and the life. If anyone believes on me, though he dies, yet he will live."[47] "For as the Father has life in himself, so he has granted the son also to have life in himself. And he has given him authority to execute judgment because he is the Son of Man. Do not be amazed at this, for an hour is coming when all who are in the tombs will hear his voice and come out, those who have done good to the resurrection of life and those who have done evil to the resurrection of judgment."[48] "For this is the will of my Father, that everyone who looks on the Son and believes in him should have eternal life, and I will raise him up at the last day."[49] The apostle Paul taught:

"For if we have been united with him (Christ) in a death like his, we shall certainly be united with him in a resurrection like his.[50]

These words of comfort and many others like them give assurance and hope to those who have faith in Christ. They convey peace for this life and promise for the next. "The Christian message grows from an honest confrontation with death that moves beyond the historical event to the spiritual meaning of the event. It is a bold affirmation of faith concerning the spiritual nature of life."[51] It is perhaps the most audacious act of faith that has grown from belief in the truth of God's promises. The reality of the resurrection emboldened the early church. "It changed the disciples from a disordered group of frightened men to a band of fearless inspired leaders."[52]

Instead of standing silent and stunned before the tragedy of death, Christians may see the funeral as an occasion for an audacious affirmation of faith. It is not a time for denial. It is a time for facing the reality of death at the physical level, and at the same moment reaffirming the promises of God regarding the resurrection of the body and continued everlasting life. Death is not the end; it is a deplorable interruption that causes great pain; but it is not a time of hopelessness; it is a time to express hope that is based on God's word. It is a time when gathered mourners may give expression to their Bible-based conviction, so outrageous to the secular world, that the person being funeralized will live again! That person, whose body is temporarily vacated by the spirit, will one day stand alive and vigorous. Her body will not be characterized by the ravages of time and illnesses, but will be strong and beautiful beyond imagination.

A Time Of Celebration?

Is a death a time for celebration? Oates' comment reflects a prevailing sentiment: "the funeral itself is a time of mourning and a time of celebration of the life of the deceased with the accent on the celebration."[53] Shall we force ourselves to embrace this fiction? Instead of facing reality squarely, death is often trivialized by these "celebrants" by overlooking its true significance. Some who have lost loved ones try to find a kind of therapeutic benefit from focusing on the pleasant things in the life of the departed. It is almost as if they imagine: "By all means, let us not think of anything that makes us feel pain or sadness. Let us think thoughts of the good times. Let us recall the legacy left and the contributions made. Enough of this morbid reflection on death!" It is disturbing to say the least that somehow the lightness and levity that characterizes so much of modern living should be brought to bear upon those who have lost a loved one to death. It seems contradictory to me for some grief counselors to advocate taking sufficient time to go through the entire process of grieving and at the same time to minimize the mourning that is so natural. It seems remarkably incongruous instead to emphasize celebration.

We should not trivialize the life of the one we lost by stressing celebration. Do those who have lost a loved one really want to celebrate? Really! Don't they feel the force of the immense inconsistency, the glaring incongruity? Their souls tell them to mourn but society tells them to celebrate. A death has taken place and it hurts. It tears at the heart and soul; it leaves the mourners diminished at several levels. And what of those whose lives that seemed characterized by difficulties and miseries? Some have experienced a deplorable existence; some have barely lived at all and have left a legacy of sorrow only. Some have suffered with debilitating diseases and limited physical and mental abilities. Some have experienced little but mental and physical affliction in their brief lives. Some have had shattered lives due to tragic losses of their own. Some have lived wasted and hurtful lives. How can mourning be turned into celebration under these circumstances? Yet, in an effort to avoid the harshness of death and the true cause of death, people will "celebrate" the life of the departed and shun mourning. Rightly did the Preacher declare: "For everything there is a season and a time for every matter under heaven. (There is) a time to mourn and a time to dance;"[54] and again: "It is better to go to the house of mourning than to go to the house of feasting, for this is the end of all mankind, and the living will lay it to heart. Sorrow is better than laughter, for by sadness of face the heart is made glad. The heart of the wise is in the house of mourning, but the heart of fools is in the house of mirth."[55]

Having made the point that celebration cannot and should not replace mourning, I affirm also that room should be made for the thankful expression to God for lives of departed loved ones. We can express our gratitude as well to the family members of the deceased, for the good influence and friendship of one no longer with us. Indeed, believers mourn, but they do not mourn as those who have no hope."[56] It is an odd paradox that people can be sorrowful and joyful at the same time. There is an appropriate "time to weep and a time to laugh; a time to mourn and a time to dance,"[57] and at death those times may overlap. One may, however, look forward to a time when God "will wipe away every tear from their eyes and death shall be no more, neither shall there be mourning nor crying, nor pain anymore, for the former things have passed away."[58]

Chapter Nine

What Is Next?

All of the days ordained for me were written in your book before one of them came to be. (Psalm 139:16 NIV)

When Everyone Has Left

After the funeral I needed to decompress. That might sound like the wrong choice of wording, but that is exactly what I did. Part of the decompressing involved simply getting away from the house and locations where the recent events had taken place. I had been under a great deal of pressure and strain especially during the four months prior to Grace's death. I simply wanted and needed to slow down and do nothing for a few days. For me, that is difficult since I seem always to be involved in something. My choice was to be involved in nothing for a little while. Yet, after about three days of relaxing, my mind drew me to the matters to which I needed to attend.

So, I went to stay with my daughter 400 miles away from where my wife and I had lived for thirty years. It was the right decision under the circumstances. I knew, and my daughter knew, that I had to get away. There had been no close relatives in the immediate area and I would have been very much alone in a large house, constantly confronted with memories. I had cared for my wife in that house during the last six weeks of her hospice. I had become emotionally and physically exhausted, numb and readily agreed to my daughter's suggestion. I needed a break from the all-too-familiar.

Follow-up

Even before the funeral service, I had received several kind expressions of sympathy and Christian concern. During the first week or so that I stayed with my daughter, I wanted to address some of the matters that remained in connection with the funeral services. In the evening hours I had ample opportunity to do just that. I expected that there would be those who would want to make some kind of memorial contributions, so with the public death notice I had designated a specific cause to which memorial contributions might be made. Several people made donations to that cause. I had purchased cards so I could send a "Thank You" to any person who made a contribution in my wife's memory. I determined to send handwritten notes to anyone who had made a memorial gift. Within a week and a half of the funeral I had all those notes written and sent. This was part of what I had tasked myself to do after the funeral. It simply is common courtesy to respond to the generosity of others. If you are anticipating the death of your wife, you may expect that you will receive such expressions and it is only right to reply to them with a proper acknowledgement in written form. This, as well, is part of what needs to be considered in anticipating the death of one's wife. Responding to the well-wishes of concerned friends and relatives is the proper and responsible thing to do. It is one of the things to which you must give your attention after matters have settled down from the flurry and frenzy of the funeral.

Another milestone which I determined to attain was the disposal of all of the sympathy cards that came to me in connection with my wife's passing. There was a pile of them. I told myself that I did not need to linger over each card but, in fact, I did reread each card and the hand written expressions of sympathy and concern one last time; then I discarded them.

Relocation

Over the years, my wife and I had visited my daughter and her family. We had considered living near her as one of our possible retirement options. We had even done some initial house searching in that area. So, I packed up what I would need for a two-week stay, and made the trip. While I was there, I realized that I would eventually come to live somewhere near my daughter. Moving would be a major step. A major transition like relocation would involve finding new grocery stores, dry cleaners, a bank, drugstores, hardware stores, shopping centers, church, dentist, restaurants, etc. It would involve attending to legal matters: placing our car into my ownership, getting a new driver's license, car registration, insurance adjustments, voter registration, arranging for utilities providers, etc., etc. One forgets how much is in place and how much has to be undone or redone.

During my two-week stay, and at my daughter's suggestion, my daughter and I looked at condo possibilities for me. It seems that, based upon popular wisdom, I did many unwise things after my wife died. It's conventional advice: "Don't make any big decisions during the first year after a spouse dies." [I have given this advice myself!] "Don't quit your job, don't sell your home, don't move; don't make any major purchases!"[1] I didn't follow my own advice and the advice of some others.

Two years earlier, my wife and I had been close to purchasing a condo in a development that we both liked, which was near my daughter's home. My daughter and I drove through that development, finding only one property for sale. We called the listing agent just to see what was being offered. The agent was free to show the property within about twenty minutes of our call. As it turned out, the property had been on the market for a couple of months, and in spite of several viewings and several open houses, there had been no offers. The unit was basically sound, but it was thirty-five years old, with just two prior owners. It needed upgrades and major cosmetic improvements. The showing ended and the realtor left with the encouragement for us to, "Think about it." A little later that day my daughter asked, "Dad, what *do* you think about it?"

I reviewed the updates that the place needed, but admitted that I liked it and its location and said to my daughter, "Let's do it." I made an offer and it was quickly accepted. An inspection was arranged and within two weeks of my wife's funeral, I had contracted to buy a condo. It might seem that I was in a hurry to make a decision, but I just didn't want to mull over a decision that, at base level, I wanted to make.

I still owned a house 400 miles away. Scheduled personal concerns there brought me back to my home town. I booked a flight to return with the intention of renting a large truck in order to bring several things back to my "new" condo. A friend lent me the use of his pickup truck while I was in town. There was a local realtor/contractor who had purchased homes in the town's historic district where Grace and I had lived. While I was still at my daughter's home, I had called him and had arranged a meeting to show my house. He knew of my property. In fact, he had lived across the street from it as a child. We met. He inspected the house and made an offer – a cash deal, no contingencies, no inspections – an "as is" offer. I thanked him, consulted with my daughter, and made a counter offer. He said he'd have to think about it and talk it over with his wife. The next day he accepted my offer. A day later we were going over a sales contract in my dining room. The house came under contract within three days of the initial meeting with the buyer! Providence all! Houses in that neighborhood had been on the market for upwards of three years without so much as a showing. My home was never on the market, but was under contract within three days. The purchaser wanted to rent my home and asked how much time I would need before I could vacate completely. I told him, "Ten days." So, I sold my house within eight weeks of my wife's funeral, disregarding conventional wisdom. As it turned out, however, the decision and its timing were providentially correct.

Plans had to change. Instead of renting a smaller truck for transporting some things to my new living quarters, I would have to secure the largest straight truck possible and clear my house completely. Instead of having time leisurely to select items to move, I had agreed to a ten-day window in which time I would need to leave the house never returning to it. I also had a two-car garage and a full basement to declutter, and I had to sell my wife's car. Needless to say, several decisions had to be made quickly – what to discard, what to keep. That task in itself often overwhelms a grieving spouse. There were so many memories attached to what had been purchased, owned and enjoyed together. There were so many "finds" and acquisitions that had been made over the years. It was difficult to break up a household simply to downsize, not to mention the added stress of having lost a loved one.

Providentially, my wife and I had performed a major reduction of her wardrobe prior to her first hospitalization. Several "loads" of clothing had found their way to local thrift stores and charitable organizations. Grace and I had lived in that house for thirty years and there was a corresponding accumulation. My approach to this rather daunting task was to decide first of all what I did not want or need. This category included furniture, small appliances, clothing, home accessories and decorations, tools and supplies of various kinds. Once I had identified what had to go, I made multiple trips to the area resale and thrift shops to transfer ownership. Some furniture made it only as far as the designated garbage pickup area. One of my neighbors claimed particular pieces of furniture and a trove of tools. Another neighbor bought Grace's car.

On return trips from making my "donations," I would secure boxes for packing, bubble wrap, tape and twine to prepare the remaining goods for transport. I worked eighteen-hour days to meet my agreed-upon deadline, but I experienced a kind of energy that was supplied for the task. Toward the end of the week after the house sale was sealed, my older son came into town to help me complete the packing and to clean the house. The church I had served called a "work day" which was to be at my home. On a Saturday, ten men loaded the truck with my selected worldly possessions. That effort took around five hours. The house was given a final sweeping; there was one last "give-away," and when the men left, I drove the truck 400 miles to my new home.

In my absence, my daughter attended to all the required legal matters to complete the condo purchase. By the time I returned, the closing had taken place. Through this entire move I was grateful for the clear superintendence of God – complications seemed to vanish, all worked out – his supply of strength and the support of his people. One might ask if all the activity aided in dealing with my grief or if it amounted to a kicking the can down the road and the answer is "Yes". There were reflective quiet moments even during that time of high activity, but the real force of grief would come later. God was and continues to be my strength and source of peace.

AFTER

Chapter Ten

Unanticipated Death

Man does not know his time. (Ecclesiastes 9:12)

Without a doubt, most deaths are to some extent anticipated. Dr. Peter Saul has emphasized that it is relatively rare for someone without any indications of sickness whatsoever, to die suddenly. Death is most often the result of a prolonged assault of a disease and the wearing down of one's ability to withstand a continued assault.[1] Perhaps an individual has a routine checkup and diagnostic tests reveal a medical condition that, if left untreated, may be life threatening. Perhaps that individual develops a disorder, becomes ill and that illness complicates that condition. Medical advice is sought and measures are taken to cure the disease or to retard its progress and to promote the health of the person who is ill. With proper care, the person improves and gets better – or not. And if not, there has been a breakdown and the likelihood of that person becoming ill with the same or similar disease has increased.

That is what took place in my wife's case. Her illness and our grief extended well over a decade. As it turned out, that was the case for all of those who agreed to be interviewed for this writing. There was a condition, a problem that became worse and complications that led eventually to the death of their wives. There was a growing awareness by each man that something was becoming seriously medically wrong with his wife. In chapter three I mentioned anxious concerns about a spouse's health. "When someone we love is diagnosed with a terminal illness, we begin our grieving process before the death. It's called anticipatory grief."[2] The men whom I interviewed came to anticipate the death of their wives and, in so doing, began to grieve about what they were losing and what they would finally lose.

Anticipatory grief has been called a double grief, "the grief of a person dying with a long-term grief over his or her gradual loss of life due to a terminal illness such as cancer and the grief of the family and close friends of the dying person."[3] In the case of a dying wife, the wife goes through the loss of strength, energy, abilities, social interaction, and overall decline while the husband can do little more than watch and pray. He too, experiences the grief of that loss even before his wife dies. "There has been an increasing awareness, voiced in psychological research literature, that it is *not* necessarily a sudden death of a spouse that causes the greater grief and adjustment difficulties for the surviving partners. Rather, there is some evidence of a prolonged decline causing more severe grief for the widow or widower and increasing the rise of post-traumatic adjustment difficulties."[4]

Accidental Death

There is, however, unanticipated death which gives no warning and for which there is no preparation. If you anticipated the death of your wife, you (and she) could grieve "in 'installments' over a preparatory period of time. A sudden bereavement comes more as a 'thief in the night' and has more damaging physiological effects."[5] Our loved ones may die in their sleep due to a condition they have that is unknown to them; they may die as a result of an accident, or a natural catastrophe; they may die due to the violence of others against them or to violence against themselves. These kinds of deaths compound and complicate the grief of the survivors. A sudden, unexpected death may bring its own kind of sorrow. The shock and sorrow crash upon the survivors in overwhelming trauma.

There are accidents every day and no one can fully avoid them. Sometimes they are explained as someone being in the wrong place at the wrong time. Accidents take place in the home and in the workplace, during recreation and travel. They leave the survivors stunned and confused, beside themselves to account for what has taken place. There may be no one morally responsible for what has occurred and no one upon whom to place any blame. It may become clear "What" has taken place, but the "Why" questions will never be satisfied.

It is well to acknowledge the inscrutability of the situation and come to terms sooner rather than later that there will be no answers in this life to explain the events that took the life of your loved one. We do live in a fallen world and we are subject to all the miseries of life in this age. This is part of the human condition.

Violence Of Others.

Unless you live by yourself on a hidden island, you are subject to violence; and then you would not be entirely able to escape violence because even then you may be liable to self-violence. As long as we live, we are "subject to all the miseries of this life," including death.[6]

Perhaps your wife met with a violent death at the hands of another. The Bible has something to say to everyone about a violent death. It makes clear that all evil in this age is due to the rebellion of our first parents when they disobeyed God's command about not eating from the Tree of the Knowledge of Good and Evil. Whether you believe that record or not, corruption and evil are pandemic. Hatred and violence come from within all members of humanity. They are expressed in various ways. To make this point, Jesus used an illustration from Jewish dietary laws about so-called clean and unclean food.

The Jewish people since the time of Moses were very careful about their diet. God's law forbade eating of *unclean* animals, and went to lengths to describe and to define what animals the people were permitted to eat.[7] When Jesus was explaining about "clean and unclean" food, he was responding to a situation that reflected cultural and religious beliefs of the Jewish people. He said, "Whatever goes into a person from the outside cannot defile him . . . What comes out of a person is what defiles him. For from within, out of the heart of man come evil thoughts, sexual immorality, theft, murder, adultery, coveting, wickedness, deceit, sensuality, envy, slander, pride, foolishness. All these evil things come from within, and they defile a person."[8] Hatred, anger, pride and jealousy give rise to acting out those thoughts. The act of murder has murderous, hateful thoughts as its source. Yet, whether directed against another person specifically or depersonalized and directed at a group bearing a cultural or ethnic identity, these thoughts are not forced upon anyone. Acts of violence may be perpetrated by individuals who have not *expressed* hatred or other passions against anyone, but their (e)valuation of others moves them to act violently.

The record of the first murder comes early in the biblical account. Genesis chapter four relates the tragic story of Cain murdering his brother Abel.[9] We are not informed about there being other brothers or sisters in that first family though probably there were. The Bible chose to focus on that first horrendous act of the taking of a human life. Anger brought about violence. Cain *planned* to kill his brother. His act was premeditated. It was what we would term "first-degree murder". Certainly, deaths occur that are not planned or intended. Accidental death from whatever causes, criminal negligence, acts of God – all sadly take the life of someone who was loved. This brief volume is not the place to delve into the workings of the heart – the envy, jealousy, fear, and pride – that can spur one to take the life of another. I note only that we in the United

States live in an increasingly violent society. In the year 2017, 1,247, 321 violent crimes took place and that figure was actually down from the year before.[10]

TV violence is fueling the fury of our young people. Our teens will have seen over 200,000 acts of violence on their screens this year. Violence is at the core of many video "games" that our children "play" over and over again.[11] It is not my place nor my point to comment on the psychological effects of TV, cinema, and home screen interaction. The debate about their effects continues, but considering what not only our young people, but the viewing public is taking in generally, is it any wonder that violence and murder rates are so staggering? Many factors contribute to the violent behavior that characterizes much of our society, however.

If you have lost your wife due to a murder or other violence, such as an auto or industrial accident, or a drug overdose, or to "an act of God," my heart goes out to you. You have all the sorrows of someone who lost his wife to a prolonged illness, but more, you carry the weight of an anguish unimaginable. You wonder about the circumstances and the particular horrors your wife may have endured. You can't help but think of her last moments, the pain she may have suffered. And if you were not present when she died, you have the added emotional stress of dealing with a false guilt of not being there to help her. There is much that you do not know and perhaps that you will never know about the circumstances of her death.

Your anguish is indescribable and something inside you cries out "Why God, Why," and possibly at the same moment you experienced irrepressible anger. You want the person(s) responsible for your wife's death to be punished. You are right in these feelings because God himself is angry with those who commit such crimes. Each person is an image-bearer of God, and murder is an assault on God as well. The feelings you have for vengeance are natural; it would be unnatural if you didn't have them. What you do with those thoughts makes all the difference in the world. God has instituted human government and its agencies to deal with lawbreakers. Early in the biblical account in Genesis we may find God's directions regarding those who commit murder: "Whoever sheds the blood of man, by man shall his blood be shed, for God made man in his own image."[12] That text suggests that man would be acting as God's agents of vengeance in such cases. The apostle Paul reminded Christians in the City of Rome that the civil authorities are God's servants, his avengers who carry out his anger against wrongdoers. Those civil authorities wield a sword and they do so for the purpose of punishing lawbreakers.[13] We do not have the prerogative of carrying out private justice. That is clear from what the apostle had written earlier: " . . . Never avenge yourselves, but leave it to the wrath of God, for it is written, 'Vengeance is mine; I will repay,' says the Lord."[14] We are not permitted to take matters into our own hands even if we could. We are not to "play God". This is extremely difficult, especially when it feels like someone has torn your wife away from you violently. We understand both from God's word and from our own experience that the wheels of justice turn slowly, and sometimes justice delayed *is* justice deferred. People do get away with murder and hundreds of lesser crimes in this age. Sometimes the law is unfair to certain classes of people and sometimes it is applied inequitably. People do not get what they deserve in this life. The best laws are imperfectly applied and judgments for violations of those laws are imperfectly applied.

At other times, the guilty are never discovered. There are no arrests, charges, trials, or judgments. We would have great cause for hopeless despair if justice in this life were all that there were. The word of God, however, points all people to the inevitable and unavoidable "Day of Judgment" when all wrongs will be righted. Nearly every book of the Bible specifically states or alludes to a time when God – the perfect judge – will call all people to account for what they have done during their lives. The apostle Paul reminded and encouraged the Christians in the City of Corinth with these words: "For we must all appear before the judgment seat of Christ, so that each one may receive what is due for what he has done in the body, whether good or evil."[15] Similarly, the writer of the Book of Hebrews explained that: "It is appointed for man to die once, and after that comes judgment."[16]

All of this factual information may bring little comfort *right now while* you grieve. The intensity of your volatile emotions may not allow you to think clearly about whatever has triggered your emotions. That's to be expected, but the time for dealing with the pressing urgencies of your wife's death will come to an end. In your more reflective moments, remind yourself of the perfect justice of God. Leave room for his righteous anger. Be assured that it will come!

Violence Against One's Self

When death is violent, whether that violence is self-inflicted or other inflicted, the shock and sorrow are compounded. Death by suicide has increased dramatically over the last fifteen years in the United States and it has increased most notably among women ages 34-65 – up twenty-four per cent during that period.[17]

I personally have known two men who have lost their wives to suicide. Their losses crushed them. They carried a sorrow they could not express. I recently attended a multiple-week seminar for those grieving the loss of a loved one. Two out of the twenty participants had lost someone due to suicide. The proliferation of illicit drug use is no small contributing factor to these deaths. It is not my intention to go into this matter, but the opioid epidemic is at crisis levels in some parts of this country. To be sure, some deaths that may have been thought suicide, may in fact have not been intentional at all, but due to drug overdoses.

If your wife took her life, you are going through and will continue to experience emotional pain and sorrow that seems nearly impossible to understand. Death may have come to be viewed as "natural" or a part of life, but death by suicide seems utterly unnatural. It is violence against one's self. It bears indelibly on the lives of those loved ones left behind. We must be frank and forthright; suicide is a violation of the sixth commandment: "You shall not murder." Suicide is the intentional, premeditated killing of one's self. Having said that, we must consider that the victim of suicide may not have been thinking correctly about his or her intended action. We must wonder if the suicide victim was thinking correctly when (s)he ended life.

The Bible relates only five instances of suicide. Each instance reflects a profound sense of desperation and hopelessness. The first and second recorded instances of suicide in the Bible are those of Israel's first King, King Saul, and his armor bearer. The Israelites were in a heated battle with the Philistines. Israel was soundly defeated and King Saul feared that if he were captured, the Philistines would torture and mutilate him. To spare himself that torture, he ordered his armor bearer to kill him. When the armor-bearer refused, King Saul fell on his own sword and died; and when Saul's armor bearer saw that the king was dead, he too fell on his own sword and died with him.[18]

The third instance is found in the Book of 1 Kings, chapter sixteen. Zimri, the fifth king of the divided Kingdom of Israel, had conspired to kill his predecessor. The armies of Israel recognized Zimri's treachery and surrounded the city where he lived. When Zimri realized the unavoidable, that he was about to be killed by his own troops, he retreated to the citadel of the king's house, and "burned the king's house over him with fire and died."[19]

The fourth instance is associated with the monarchy of King David. Toward the end of his reign, King David's son Absalom led a rebellion to overthrow his father. Absalom had led a conspiracy against his father and had established a headquarters in the City of Hebron. While he was there, he summoned one of David's advisers, Ahithophel, and gained his support. David fled Jerusalem but left one of his faithful counselors, Hushai, in Jerusalem who would advise Absalom in ways that would be of an advantage to David. When Absalom and his army came to Jerusalem, he asked the counselors whether he should pursue his father immediately or to wait in order to build the strength of his army, and then to pursue David later. Absalom took Hushai's counsel instead of Ahithopel's. Ahithophel went to his house, set his house in order and hanged himself.[20]

Of course, the most infamous suicide is that of Judas Iscariot, the betrayer of Jesus Christ. For thirty pieces of silver, Judas had bargained to hand Jesus over to the Jewish religious leadership. He received his money and in the Garden of Gethsemane made good on his agreement.[21] After Jesus was tried and condemned, Judas changed his mind and tried to return the betrayal money. The chief priests and the elders didn't care about Judas' remorse. Judas threw the 30 pieces of silver into the temple. He left and hanged himself.[22]

In all of those accounts, suicide was the action taken by someone who had been hopelessly desperate, who, with a narrow focus saw no other course of action. Now, of course, there were other courses of action they could have taken, but suicide was the only option they saw at the time. With a very limited view, they were convinced that their choice was better than staying alive and facing their situations. Their suicides were acts of desperation.

In some respects, all suicides are acts of desperation. For reasons known only to those who take their own lives – or perhaps not known to them – their situations loom so insurmountably "hopeless" that they see no other solution to their pain, condition, or difficulty than to end their lives. They must think of their individual cases as beyond remedy.

If your wife ended her life in this way, you will certainly experience compounded grief. You very well may be overwhelmed with feelings of guilt, asking yourself why you didn't "see this coming," or why you didn't see the signs. You may be troubled with "if only" questions – "If only I had listened more attentively; if only I had picked up on the signals; if only I had spoken words of hope and encouragement more often than I did; if only I had not been so critical or cold; if only..." You fill in the blank. Perhaps you feel indirectly responsible for your wife's action. You should not feel that way. Your influence was not the *only* influence upon your wife; your words were not the *only* words she heard; your interactions with her were not the *only* interaction she had. Many things past – distant and recent – may have contributed to the way your wife viewed her situation; may have shaped her beliefs and opinions. What she read, what she saw, what she experienced – all may have affected her decision. Don't blame yourself or anyone else for that matter for what happened.

There also is a stigma attached to the suicide of your spouse. You may ask yourself if you contributed to her action; if you were the kind of support and comfort that you should have been; if you were there when she needed you to be there. In days ahead you will have to deal with the thoughts that those around you might be thinking the very same things. You can't control what other people think about your experience; you can control only what you think and what you say in your grief. Remember, that you are to give glory to God in your grieving no matter how your wife died.

You may be angry at your loved one for leaving as she did; you may be angry at God for allowing something like this to happen. Remember, that improper anger will not help you heal and may actually prolong your grief. Anger is not the route to peace; it does not assist in bringing about the righteous life God desires, no matter to whom it may be directed.[23]

What is more, you will not be able to figure out "why". The reason(s) "why" were probably not known even to the one who ended her life in this way. Don't torture yourself by trying to discover reasons why. "Answers" in your situation are not found in uncovering details of your late wife's inner thinking. You cannot do it in any case. Decide that you will be satisfied in never knowing "why," and seek the peace and comfort that comes from God alone. I'm not suggesting a mystical experience. God chooses to work through agents and means. Go to people who will truly listen to your confusion and then point you to the Ultimate Comfort. Use the means that God has determined for you to use to bring you closer to him! Read his word slowly, deliberately, and make it personal. Ask God to heal your broken heart and to comfort your troubled mind. God alone can and will do this!

Perhaps you are someone who wishes to help a man whose wife ended her life in this way. "If someone you know is trying to cope with such a loss, don't ask too many questions. People have a morbid curiosity about this kind of death, and it is unfair to constantly place grieving family members in the position of explaining the death. On the other hand, if the person opens up voluntarily, just listen and give support . . . When a griever is in 'search mode' looking for answers after a death, allow . . . [that individual] the time and space to do this without added guilt."[24] Be a good listener and point that person to the mercies and comforts God offers in his word.

One final thought about suicide and one's standing before God – some have taught that suicide is virtually the unpardonable sin. After all, a person who takes his own life has committed first-degree murder and by that act has removed any possibility of repentance. That person appears before God, it is thought, with an unforgiven sin on his record. Let me ask candidly: do you really think that at the point of your death you will be lucid enough to search the recesses of your mind and the depths of your heart in order to confess all your known sin, so that you will not appear before God with unconfessed sin? Would you even be able to do this with a completely clear mind?

What if a person were to lose life in a car accident or in a natural catastrophe; what if a person were to ease into death after a prolonged coma? Would people in those conditions and situations have the capacity or even the opportunity to confess all known sins? The clear answer is "No". What if you with the clearest of mind were to spend hours in confession and were to scour your mind for any known sin. Would you in your finitude be convinced that you identified them all? Then, think of the sins of which you have no knowledge at all (not knowing one's sin does not thereby nullify it). Would you be able to stand before the infinitely holy God as sin free? The obvious answer is "No". One person alone stands before the holiness and justice of God perfectly pure and perfectly holy. He is Jesus Christ, the righteous One.[25]

One's standing before God does not depend upon whether or not he or she is able to confess all sin – known or otherwise – but is based upon one's relationship to God in and through union with Christ. By virtue of Christ's death to pay for the sins of all of his people, those who are indeed his people do not have to concern themselves about whether they happen to have every known sin confessed at the time of death. This is a blessed assurance: those who are in union with Christ appear before God as though they had ***never*** sinned. Those who take their own life, if they are in Christ, appear before God as righteous as Christ. Their thinking may have been clouded at the time of their death; their evaluations of the desperate situation in which they found themselves may have been entirely wrong, but they have no bearing on their standing before God.

With this clear understanding, a believer does not need excessively to grieve about this point; does not need to have thoughts of his loved one being eternally lost, but rather that if your wife had faith in God through Christ, she is in the presence of God without any sin or sorrow!

Chapter Eleven

What Is New

There is a time to weep and a time to laugh; a time to mourn and a time to dance. (Ecclesiastes 3:4)

Routine

Over the years you and your wife came to an understanding about how the household should operate. Both of you assumed and became specialists in your particular roles. You may have done the greater share of the cooking but she may have enjoyed taking care of the yard. You perhaps attended to medical and insurance issues, whereas your wife became expertly involved in the banking. Maybe you planned celebrations or vacations together but she maintained the social calendar and you handled the car maintenance. It may be that your wife was the chief administrator as many wives are. Whatever your unique arrangements had been, you now will have to add her responsibilities to those which were yours. As I suggested earlier in chapter three, you will have to know, perhaps for the first time *what* needs to be done. You are probably not aware of all those little duties she performed in order to keep the household running smoothly. You will decide if you are able or willing to do that specific work. For example, Grace took care of all the banking, bill paying, insurance, taxes and retirement matters; she was able to keep on top of it all. In her absence, I have assumed the banking, bill paying and insurance side of things, but realize that I was not able realistically to manage the taxes and retirement funds. I committed those responsibilities to a reliable agency.

Studies have been explored on the difficulties faced by those who have lost their spouses. Aside from dealing with the loneliness, which both men and women identified as their primary concern during the first two years of bereavement, both "men and women reported that . . . completing the tasks of daily living was their second most difficult problem. The difference emerged in their specific tasks of daily life. As expected . . . bereaved widowers aged 50 and over were having great difficulty in shopping, preparing meals, and managing the household. The widows expressed having major problems doing home repairs, managing financial and legal matters, and taking care of their automobiles."[1]

My wife and I shared the shopping, housekeeping and cooking responsibilities. Toward the end of her life, she was not able to be involved in any of these. I assumed them and continue to do those duties. If you have adult children, perhaps they can help with some of the tasks that your wife so ably performed. Don't hesitate to ask for help. Admit to your inability or disinclination to perform specific tasks. Perhaps you could learn them over time, but you are currently uncomfortable doing them. That's perfectly fine. Get some help. Ask!

Holidays, family gatherings, special Days and Dates

The issues of "emotional triggers" and times of the year that are especially difficult, frequently come into discussion about coping with the loss of a loved one. Most people, whether they are grieving a loss or not, have memories of special dates and events in their lives which evoke an emotional response in them. Vacations, birthdays, holidays and milestones you have experienced as a family bring back tender memories of the one(s) you have lost to death. Friends and family will certainly ask questions about how you are going to do on the anniversaries of those special occasions. "Firsts" are tough. If your wife passed away near Thanksgiving Day, for example, you will inevitably think about your wife's passing each time Thanksgiving Day comes around. If you and your wife took a special trip and purchased a commemorative item of that adventure, each time you look at it, you will be reminded of your wife and that trip. Annual family gatherings will continue, but in years ahead, your dearly-loved one will not be present. Thoughts of your wife's birthday, your wedding anniversary and other dates that meant so much to both of you may bring about a very sad and tearful time. Be prepared for these events. Understand that being with family and friends on a holiday, minus one, may make you very emotionally uncomfortable.

Several of the men I interviewed expressed their thoughts about emotional triggers they face.

[T]alking about her and it happens. So I guess verbally talking about her with someone or in front of people still causes sadness. Usually on the holidays and whenever those came about, my family was all around me. We didn't talk enough about Carol at those family [gatherings]; well in fact, we almost never did at all. I should have been more free [with] them to talk about [her]. So, I should've spoken

about her and let them talk then. Holidays are lonely. I go [to family gatherings] by myself and came back myself but [I was] not as emotional after a time. RP

They're just more memories . . . My wife kept a scrapbook and she had pictures [all] over the place with various papers . . . going through them I get sad. [But] at some of those times I'm happy about having the memories. I am grateful for the years [we had]. I would like to have had more. I realize that I [will] have no more so I'm sad. I miss her, but I'm not debilitated by it. If something does trigger [my emotions], I try to live [in] that moment and accept it and not try to run from it. WZ

Christmas time is a tough one for me. I usually travel to be with my daughter. LL

There are many triggers. Just being alone is sorrowful. I thought that perhaps watching television would help me, but it does not help. ZB

These times are difficult! My wife passed away on the twenty-third of the month. The funeral was one week later on the thirtieth. I proposed marriage to my wife on the thirtieth. Our oldest son was married on the thirtieth. Those dates – twenty-third and thirtieth – come around (nearly) every month. When they do, I can't help but recall what I was doing on those dates. I stated that I had proposed marriage to my wife on the thirtieth as well. That date had marked a very happy occasion for me and for the one who would become my wife. We would move forward together no matter what obstacles or difficulties. We would be together. We were committed to each other "for better or for worse". The marriage ceremony made it official of course but the agreement was privately pledged on the thirtieth. What irony! an engagement and a funeral. Yes, I will not forget the thirtieth!

Actually, our marriage *ceremony* took place later that year on the thirty-first of the month. This date as well will stick in my mind. Somehow those days and months and years end up being security codes, cell phone numbers and passwords in this technological age. If not changed, they serve as routine reminders of a relationship that has ended.

What was initially rough for me was the close proximity of both of our birthdays and our wedding anniversary. Within fifteen days the three special days would come. In the later years of our marriage, we made it a point to be on vacation or to take a trip that would coincide with those commemorative days.

There's one more bizarre detail to this matter of dates. The final resting place for my wife is located a few blocks from where I currently reside. The purchase of the plot was not complicated and relatively (and surprisingly) inexpensive; at least the sale price was less than I had anticipated paying. I wanted to have a particularly shaped memorial stone and I discovered that there were just three remaining sites in the entire cemetery where such a monument could be placed. My daughter and I made a self-tour of the cemetery and decided on the gravesite. Several weeks passed and I thought it well to purchase an appropriate marker. Conversations with the people at the monument company were cordial and uncomplicated. I had selected a passage from Second Corinthians to be engraved on the stone. Because of a backlog in the work, the memorial marker would not be ready for several weeks, which, due to an ordering error, turned out to a number of months. As the time for delivery and installation of the stone approached, I was notified that the placement would be within particular work week. And so, with divine timing, the stone was delivered and positioned on my birthday! That date will have new significance for me. (I address days and dates more specifically in chapter thirteen.)

The Question of Remarriage

"There are no governmental statistics on the number of widowers who remarry. Yet the Census Bureau estimates that 10 times as many widowers as widows over 65 remarry, though there are fewer older men than older women. Whether widowers remarry at a higher rate than divorced men is difficult to say. No official statistics are kept of that either. But marriage counselors believe that widowers are more likely to remarry than divorced men. 'For men whose marriage ends only because of death there is often a desire to repeat the happiness they knew.'"[2]

I mentioned earlier that Grace made a firm statement that she wanted me to remarry after her death. The Bible certainly approves of it under the specific condition that a believer in Christ must marry someone who is a believer in Christ. That condition bears on Christians who want to marry whether they have been married before or not. Marriage for a Christian must be to another Christian. What the apostle Paul wrote about in chapter seven of First Corinthians bears directly on this matter: "A wife is bound to her husband as long as he lives. But, if her husband dies, she is free to be married to whom she wishes, only in the Lord."[3] A marriage is legally and practically ended when either husband or wife dies. We might even say that God has ended the marriage since in his sovereignty, he took the life of one in the marriage. The biblical law regulating marriage is no longer binding upon the surviving spouse. Consequently, he or she is free to marry again.

The apostle Paul provided essentially the same instruction when he wrote to the Christians in the City of Rome, "Or do you not know brothers – for I am speaking to those who know the law – that the law is binding on a person only as long as he lives? Thus a married woman is bound by the law to her husband while he lives, but if her husband dies she is released from the law of marriage . . . But if her husband dies, she is free from that law and if she marries another man, she is not an adulteress."[4] Legally and morally it is perfectly acceptable for one whose marriage partner has died to remarry.

There are, however, other considerations about remarriage of a more social, familial, and personal nature. Age difference could be one such consideration. (This is also something to think about in a first marriage.) Ask yourself, "Is there a significant age disparity that might bear on the relationship immediately and/or in the next five to ten years or longer?" I've personally known of first and second marriages in which there was significant age difference and the marriages are working well! Nevertheless, as in a first marriage and so more likely in a second, one person will lay the other to rest. If marriage vows are taken seriously, particularly "till death do us part," this is the prospect for every married couple. No one, of course, is guaranteed good health and longevity. I've known of marriages where there has been a twenty-year age difference, and the younger has died first.

As a widower, you should think about the same issues that you did when you were attracted to your first wife: are your backgrounds fairly similar? Are your interests and lifestyles compatible? Do you enjoy the same things? Are your perspectives about life the same or similar? Are your values the same? Are you in the same place in your life? Are you both prepared to make (another) marriage commitment? Ask yourself these kinds of questions and ask them of that woman whom you may marry.

A rush to remarry can be disastrous, particularly if you have not allowed yourself to grieve sufficiently! It takes a while fully to come to terms with what has happened to you. A number of the men I interviewed admitted to being numb for the first year after the death of their wives and stated that they functioned nearly mechanically. In such a condition, it is not wise to make a decision of such great weight as remarriage. Yet, according to Heath, "Our disposable society . . . has widows and widowers remarry within a year of their partner's death, long before true healing has taken place. Unresolved grief is then carried into the next marriage. Combine this with whatever other issues these two people [have], and is it any wonder most of these marriages eventually fail?"[5]

It takes time to sort things out and to begin to make adjustments mentally, socially and spiritually. The passage of time allows for a settling into a new situation and a new status. All this adjusting should not be cut short and a remarriage too soon may only stall, and possibly complicate your adjustment. In fact, it would add to your adjustments.

The length of your grieving, particularly the intense grieving after loss of your wife varies with the nature of your relationship, your ages and other factors that may be unique to the process of grieving. There will be that vacancy in your heart for as long as you live. Even if you remarry, you will not stop loving your first wife. You will not love her in that same way to be sure, but your departed wife will always hold a special place in your heart.

Having recognized that, you should realize that people closest to you as well as people in society in general, have expectations about how long you should grieve and if you grieve for what to them seems like an inordinate length of time, people may say, "Why can't he get over this; he talks and acts as if his loss were only yesterday." On the other hand, if you don't grieve for what is popularly perceived as a sufficient length of time, there will be those who will think that you were not sorrowful long enough, that you really didn't feel the pain as you ought to have felt it. Perhaps you will be expected to speak about your loss in certain ways. But again, the way you express your grief and the length of time you grieve intensely varies, and many of the same factors that bear on an extended time of mourning, bear on what may seem to be an abbreviated time.

Family and friends are sometimes scandalized by the remarriage "too soon" of one who has lost his wife. Such was the case when my grandpa lost his wife. His wife was fifty-six when she died; he was fifty-nine. Her death was not expected; she was the picture of health – energetic, funny, and involved. Consequently, the family, and especially my grandpa, was shocked with disbelief. Grandma died of a cerebral hemorrhage. She went into a coma and didn't wake up. Nothing could be done. My grandpa was remarried at the age of sixty, less than a year after his wife's death. The family was appalled and viewed his decision as near sacrilege! How could grandpa remarry so soon after burying his dear wife? It was a near sacrilege! What kind of respect did he have for his departed wife, marrying within the year of her death? His children (my mother, aunts and uncles) were offended that their father seemed not to care enough about their mother as they expected he should have cared. He married a widow who had lost her husband several years earlier, who had adult children and grandchildren much as did he. Grandpa had known her for over twenty-five years. They had interacted on a regular basis. I think that if his children could have considered the situation objectively, they might have expected that the marriage might take place.

There was an attempt to bring the two families together through a couple of picnics, but that "blended family" never came about. The relationship between the two families was at best strained. Grandpa's children seemed not to be able to get past the idea that his new wife was a replacement for their mother. Even as a young teenager at the time, I was frankly embarrassed by some of their comments, and now I can appreciate the reasons for my grandpa's actions. He had loved his wife intensely and was extremely lonely. God had provided a very compatible widow for him to marry, who also was a member of the same congregation to which he belonged. The two of them enjoyed sixteen years of marriage before he died. If you remarry and if you or your prospective wife have children living at home, this story may help you consider some of the ramifications of having a blended family.

Some of the interviewees used a matching service; they hoped to find a wife. If you are inclined to use such a service, you might be surprised to learn that there are several of them. Such services often are specific in narrowing the field for you with respect to age, religion, etc. If you choose to use such a service, you will be asked to complete a profile of yourself — physical attributes, academic background, social interests, religious preferences, etc. and what you would desire in a prospective wife. There is a monthly charge to view the profiles of the women who meet your criteria. What you would consider a match may differ significantly from what the service would suggest, however. There are obvious advantages and disadvantages to use a matching service, but they can be used successfully as a means of bringing two people together. Of the men interviewed for this effort, three have remarried and all the interviewees have expressed a desire to be married again.

There may be those of you who are rather apprehensive about the prospect of starting over. For reasons known only to you, you wonder if the sorrow you experienced in the loss of your wife may be repeated, and you don't know if you can go through that again; or, perhaps knowing the difficulties you faced, you would not want to put a future wife though them in caring for you. In any future relationship, you will not be the inexperienced, young man you were not ever having been married before. The season of your life has changed. I offer this perspective from psychologist Kathleen O'Hara:

Often in new relationships ... survivors of a loss are afraid to love again because of the possibility of another loss. To open our hearts again is to risk being hurt again.

This is a real fear. How can we trust that it will [not] happen again? Many of us will close ourselves down instead of taking another risk ... The timing and receptivity to new relationships will be entirely up to you. Some of you may meet someone special to help you; while others of you may decide it is too soon. It is your decision to make. When you decide to enter another relationship, you will take a risk – that is the nature of love. There is no guarantee it will not hurt. In fact you [may expect that] it will. And yet, you will love again – it is important to open your heart to the possibility of the future and what relationships it will bring to you.[6]

By all means, give yourself time to heal and to adjust to your new status. Avoid carrying the grief of your loss into a new relationship. If you are considering remarriage, talk with friends about your thoughts, ask their opinions about the questions you may have. Seek advice from those who have been widowers and have remarried. Their insights will be valuable. Pray for guidance; seek that peace that knowing and doing God's will bring to you. You understand from God's word that he is sovereign in all matters. When, therefore, you ask for the guidance and assistance of God, believe that he will give them to you.

Chapter Twelve

How Do You Think About Grief?

And David lamented with this lamentation... (2 Samuel 1:17-27)

Consider the range of emotion shown by King David when he experienced the death of family members and of others who touched his life. When he discovered that his wives and children, as well as the wives and children of his followers had been taken by the Amalekites, David and his men sat down and wept until they had no more strength to weep.[1] They had not been killed, but David and his men did not know that. When he learned of the death of his dearly-loved and closest friend Jonathan, he cried out in anguished grief. He and his men mourned and wept and fasted. We would say that he had a broken heart. And even when King Saul, who had tried several times to kill him died in battle, David lamented the death of the Lord's anointed king.[2] Abner had been the renowned commander-in-chief of King Saul's army. When he was murdered, David called for his men to tear their clothes, wear sackcloth and mourn for a fallen hero. He followed the bier in a funeral procession, and wept at the gravesite. He composed a lament for Abner.[3] Ishbosheth, the son of the King Saul and presumptive heir to Israel's throne was murdered by those who thought David would be pleased by the removal of a rival. Instead, David was outraged and had the assassins executed.[4] When he heard (wrongly) that several of his sons had been killed, he wept and displayed the anguish of a bereft parent. He tore his clothing and collapsed to the ground in mourning,[5] but several years earlier when his infant son died as Nathan the prophet had predicted, David received the report of the loss with remarkable composure and worshiped God.[6] As news reached him of the death of his son Absalom, he was out of his mind with inconsolable grief.[7]

One does not have a choice as to whether he will grieve; grief is not optional. Someone has expressed it this way: Choosing not to grieve due to a loss is like deciding not to bleed after sustaining a cut. "Grief" and "mourning" are words that have been used interchangeably sometimes to mean the same thing. But, the fact is, there really is a very important difference between them. Grief is an emotional reaction/response to loss. It is internal. Grief tends to follow a common pattern of emotional states, such as shock, confusion, denial, anger, sadness, rage, depression, and isolation to name a few, and not always in that order. Grief "is the brain's way of dealing with a [traumatic loss] that it cannot completely comprehend in the moment; so it takes time to try to sort through" what has taken place.[8] It has been described as "anguish of the soul, a deep remorse over loss."[9]

There is an external aspect of grief. Grief is what a person feels; mourning is what a person shows: crying; somber facial expressions, slow and monotonal speaking, drooping posture, comments betraying a feeling of hopelessness or confusion. People see it and hear it. In our western society, wearing a black dress has been considered appropriate for women in mourning, whereas a red dress or brightly-colored dress might have been considered improper. Men used to wear a black armband to indicate that they were in mourning. In other cultures, the color white is worn to show proper respect for the dead and to indicate mourning. In virtually every culture there is an appropriate way to express grief through mourning. In fact, mourning is essentially cultural; it is learned and passed from one generation to the next; it is driven by social expectations. Presently, however, more attention seems to be given to the working of the mind in dealing with grief than to external conventions of expressing it.

Whereas, in the case of the loss of a loved one, grief is the emotional reaction/response to loss; **mourning** may be regarded as the process one undertakes to deal with the void that the loss has left. It is an adjustment to living life without that special someone. It involves a period of adapting to the changes created by loss. Both grief and mourning are important and are interrelated, even long after the loss. Although each has different roles, both play important parts in dealing with loss to help to heal one's mind, heart and soul.

Since this is a book primarily to and for widowers, we ask a question that has been asked by professional grief counselors and by those among the general public who are curious about the matter: "Do men and women grieve differently?" Many psychologists stress gender differences in grieving, but using the distinctions mentioned above, perhaps the question is better worded another way: "Do men and women mourn differently?" Both men and women have emotions; they have feelings. No one would deny this. "We do not decide whether or not we will have feelings. We have only the choice as to how wisely and well we will manage them."[10] The way they express their emotions through mourning is different.

I mentioned that mourning is cultural. In our western society, men are *expected* to mourn differently than women. "Like it or not, society still assigns different roles to men and women, and this certainly carries over into [their showing] grief. Men are supposed to be strong and take charge. People ask: 'Is your wife holding up?' and neglect to ask how he is doing. Being strong is somehow synonymous with being emotionless."[11] Yes, everyone has emotions, but the point concerns how society expects men to show their grief. Men have been socialized in ways that affect the way they show grief. "Many boys and young men are taught that tears are for babies, that crying is a sign of weakness, and that men have to be strong . . . Some men are embarrassed and apologetic if anyone sees them cry and try to keep a very tight rein on their emotions for fear that any display of their grief will be thought unmanly."[12] If men (or women) express their grief in ways that are not culturally characteristic, people take notice and comment.

Studies have shown that men and women do tend to cope with grief differently. Lund found that, "widowers spoke more about loss as 'dismemberment,' while women looked at loss in terms of abandonment."[13] Such was also indicated in comments of a couple of the interviewees:

When Lindsey died I felt like part of me had been ripped away. Half of who I am is gone. JA

After Sherri died I felt like part of me was gone, but it wasn't an overriding thought. I didn't feel my life was over. Life goes on and I know that I have to move on. EF

What's more, men tend to be more private and introspective about their grief.[14] Women tend to reflect on relationships. They are able to express emotional pain openly and are willing to accept support offered to them. On the other hand, "Men tend to be less expressive about their feelings. [They] are more likely than women to remain silent or grieve in isolation, engage in action-oriented forms of grief expression or lose themselves in [their] work."[15] They want to know what has happened to them and take action to deal with their pain. Men's styles are more likely to focus on action. Again, this was reflected in interviewee comments:

I started reading books about grief and got familiar with it because I didn't understand what was happening to me. [Italics mine] I never experienced anger. I only really experienced confusion about why God would do this . . . I never felt as though [my wife's death] was anybody's fault, just confusion about why God let it happen. My greatest trial was understanding why God let this happen to her when she was such a strong Christian woman and was healthy. RP

I was hoping that I would be able to handle it – to come to grips with and understand what had happened. In the past, I have been able to do that very well . . . I cannot answer the question, "Why in the world [my wife and I] had to be separated." I can't figure this out. I have no answer except for a very general one. JA

Men's tendency to be introspective and private may be interpreted as their lacking emotion. This perception, along with men's associated withdrawal from social contact can result in their isolation. "Men do share their losses but often in ways different than women; they often sob privately when no one is around."[16]

It would be incorrect to think that men must follow a particular pattern of mourning, however. Two men may differ in their mourning over the loss of their respective wives as greatly as any man would differ from any woman's mourning the loss of her husband. Because people are unique, no two of them will grieve alike and no two of them will mourn alike. The nature of the marriage, the length of the marriage, the age of the couple and all the rest of life's experiences bear on how one shows grief. "Someone once said that we grieve as we live. If someone is a reserved stoic in life in general, that person is likely to grieve as a reserved stoic. If someone else finds it easy to express emotion in life, then that person will be more likely to show grief by expressing emotion."[17] When reflecting on his own grief, one of the interviewees remarked:

I don't think I have grieved properly, maybe not long enough. Sometimes I feel guilty for dealing with [Sherri's death] so well. EF

I expect that the interviewee had a culturally shaped estimation of how long or in what ways he should have shown his grief. When his grieving did not match that expectation, he questioned its propriety. Who is to determine what proper grieving involves? The way in which one deals with grief is as unique as the grief itself. What standard is to be achieved or what conditions met in order for me or you or anyone else to say: "You have properly grieved."? There is not one standard that fits everyone. Certainly, there are similarities between the grieving of two people but the uniqueness of one's grief will match his uniqueness as an individual.

What About Stages of Grief?

Are there seasons or stages or phases of Grief? Many of you have heard about the so-called stages of death and dying. The name of Elizabeth Kübler-Ross has come to be associated with the psychological stages of dying. She has become an icon for those who study death and dying. Kübler-Ross was a medical doctor who, at one time in her career, lectured to medical students about what their dying patients were experiencing psychologically. To do this she conducted an interview with a terminal patient, while her students were present. Her presentation was eye-opening and touching for her students. She continued to interview dying patients at her other stopping points throughout her career. These interviews were not conducted as part of clinical studies, nor were the questions she posed to the patients in any way standardized.[18] The information was largely anecdotal. The interviewees were encouraged to speak freely about whatever came into their minds. When Kübler-Ross was asked to write a book for the Macmillan Book Company, she struggled for three weeks to formulate a concept for the book. She was convinced that every one of her dying interviewees went through similar psychological stages: denial, anger, bargaining, depression and acceptance. Konigsberg comments that, "the [presenting of the] stages of death were the result of late-night brainstorming to overcome writer's block, rather than a consistent pattern derived from explicit interviews with dying patients."[19]

These "stages" became so popularized that they had come to a status of orthodoxy in thinking of medical professionals about what the dying experience psychologically. What's more, the population generally seems to have accepted this rubric as the standard for what the dying experience. They are so ingrained in the popular thought.

It seems well at this point, to recognize that, by and large, the medical and psychological communities no longer adhere to a rigid stage theory (if they ever did). There are probably those practitioners on the periphery of medical and social work, who are not current with emerging trends, who still may refer to the stages theory in their informal counseling and in their public presentations. In any case, we are not considering what the terminally ill may experience, but what those who are grieving the death of a loved one may experience! These stages came to be applied to those in grief and grieving. How did the shift take place from applying the "stages" to those who are grieving their own deaths to applying the "stages" to those grieving the death of another? Konigsberg suggests that the responsibility, at least in part, is due to Kübler-Ross herself. In an interview, "when she could have set the world straight that her stages were for the terminally ill, she instead encouraged their misapplication, saying, 'Even though I called it the stages of dying, it is really a natural adjustment to loss.'"[20] Today, people will speak of the stages of grieving as standard parlance on the subject. Family members and friends of someone who has experienced the loss of a loved one may ask about what stage the griever is in.[21] "This can be confusing, since there are several lists that include anywhere from five to nine separate stages. You may also find it misleading, because the word 'stages' may suggest that you'll make a neat, orderly progression from one stage to another. The stages describe our reactions to the death of someone we love, and usually those reactions are not neat and orderly."[22] This statement reflects the assumption that there are identifiable stages through which a griever passes on a journey to wellness.

The term "stages" suggests a linear approach to an experience, but anyone who has lost a loved one to death knows that the experience is not a tidy transition from one emotion to another. It would be difficult enough to deal with one emotion at a time, and resolve it only to move on to the next, but grief requires that the griever deal with multiple and related emotions at the same time. Grief is anything but linear; it is not an orderly thing. Its complexities defy analysis.

Variety in Grief Expression

You know from your own experience that you may have several emotional thoughts throughout the day. You are not distinctly in a stage/phase of anger, for example, because you happen to feel anger during the day. On that very same day, you may become extremely depressed. You would not therefore say that you are in a stage of depression, but simply that you feel depressed. You may feel a wide range of emotions during any given day. I expect that someone could argue that during the different so-called stages there is an emotion that is prevalent, but the emotions that may dominate a day may be very different from day to day. You may very well experience all (or ten) emotions of the so-called stages each day.

Perhaps a way to illustrate facing the strength and variety of your emotions due to the loss of your loved one is to compare your experience to being at the ocean beach on a windy day when the waves are high. You want to get into the water and make your way some distance from the shore where the waves are less assaulting. You make your approach. You feel the rhythmic pulse of the water against you. As you continue, the water is waist high. You can see large waves coming toward you and you brace yourself for their impact. You stiffen your legs and square your body for the next wave, but then one crashes against you that you did not see. It knocks you back and you stagger only to be hit by another from a different direction that knocks you completely off your feet. Now you're underwater and you regain your bearings long enough to stand up and then you are smacked by another wave. This continues until you have swum far enough out into the water to where the upward slope of the ground to the shore no longer creates those pounding surges against your body. In a very real sense, you cannot prepare for the wave you do not see, and preparing for one surge only to be impacted by one you do not expect may increase your vulnerability to the one you do not expect. Wiant advises, "When possible, we are better off accepting the normalcy of experiencing temporary difficulties of some sort."[23]

Frequency and Intensity

Rather than to think of your grief process as linear, that moves in a predictable way toward resolution of your grief over time, it may be more helpful for you to think of it in terms of a scatter diagram. Imagine your varying emotions as represented by paint pellets of different *colors* and different *sizes*. In your hand you have several of those pellets – blue, yellow, red, orange, purple, green, etc. You gripped them tightly, then throw them as hard as you can against a canvas located six feet away. The multi-colored "buckshot" will strike a canvas and create a "splattergraph". Most of the paint will be concentrated to form a center point, but other pellets will have impacted the canvas at various distances from the center. At the impact center, the colors will be mixed so that it could be difficult to distinguish one color from another, or to tell where one color ends and another begins. It may appear that various colors have mingled to make a hue that you did not hurl.

Center indicates intense emotion at the time of death of a loved one.
Concentric circles indicate units of time.
Movement away from center suggests less frequent intense emotion.

At the point of your greatest grief, your emotions may be compared to what you would find at the center of that "splattergraph" – confused, complicated, co-mingled, and confounding. You feel really bad but it's hard to isolate the various emotions you may be experiencing all at once. You feel as though your mind wants to shut down and probably, to some extent it does. It does not process quickly all that has happened to you.

If we continue the analogy, however, we could draw concentric circles around that center point. The smaller circles near that center would have a higher concentration of various size and color paint spatters. The farther away from the center, the fewer paint pellet splatters. There would still be a variety, but the frequency of those colorful various size splatters would be reduced. If you were to assign time values to the rings around the center point – say six months to a year – you would notice that as time passes, the expression of the variety of your very real emotion does not disappear but it becomes less intense and less frequent. If you were able to expand the canvas, you would eventually not find evidence of your paint pellet experiment as you moved out from the impact center. This is one point at which the analogy breaks down however. You will always have those emotions related to the death of your wife. "Though Kübler-Ross identified acceptance as her final stage, implying some kind of end point, she also said that you could never fully close the chapter on grief. 'The reality is that you will grieve forever,' she concluded in *On Grief and Grieving* . . . 'You will not "get over" the loss of a loved one; you will learn to live with it.'"[24] At some level throughout your life you will experience emotions related to your great loss.

Another way of depicting this relationship of the frequency and intensity of the expressions of emotion to time is illustrated in the following graph. With "10" being high and "1" being low; and starting in the lower left-hand corner of the graph to indicate the loss event, we see that closer to the loss, the frequency of emotional expression and the intensity of that expression would be at a "10". We would expect that nearer to the loss of your wife, both the intensity and frequency of your emotional expression would be high. At the very start, however, you may feel nothing. You may be emotionally numb. So, the graph suggests a likely increase in your emotion expression some time after the loss. As the line moves away from the "loss event" both the intensity and frequency of emotional expression decline. I think that this model more realistically reflects the experience of those who have lost loved ones.

If you have lost your wife, you will experience a wide range of emotions and you will likely feel them intensively and frequently in grieving for her – and all that you have lost. "You may feel sad, guilty, angry, lonely, abandoned, isolated, numb, bewildered, relieved. [You may] find it difficult to identify or understand [your] reactions especially if [you] are feeling numb."[25]

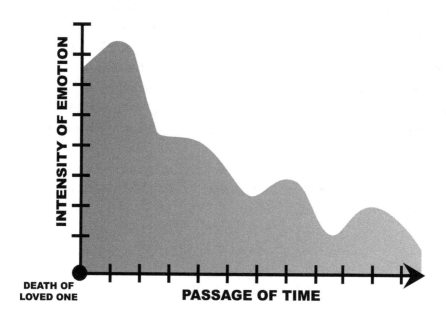

Some of the men I interviewed expressed this very thing:

I really couldn't feel a thing [after Heather's death]. I was under pressure to do many things very quickly. ZB

I was just numb at the time. I was living in my own pain at the time. I just told myself that I had to keep going. LL

I was just in a daze for weeks afterward. Sometimes I would think Sherri would pull into the driveway and ask me to help unload groceries. EF

What's more, you may find yourself feeling two *seemingly incompatible* emotions simultaneously. "Maybe you feel glad that [your wife] is no longer in pain – and angry that she left you. You may feel grateful for the assistance of your family and at the same time feel threatened by their presence. You may find that your moods shift frequently and abruptly. Perhaps you're calmly planning a service and suddenly feel overcome with sadness and tears. You may feel extremely depressed and then find yourself laughing at something funny. This emotional roller coaster seems to drain your energy."[26] These mood swings are not unusual for those who experience the grief of loss. You may repeatedly rehearse what happened without being able to make any sense of it. You may believe you hear the voice of your loved one. You are not going crazy; "over half of grieving spouses say it has happened to them."[27] Your emotions may be like a kaleidoscope, where little pieces of colored shapes form intricate patterns that change with the slightest movement. You may experience several different emotions in rapid succession or simultaneously. Each change effects a shift in the pattern. This can be overwhelming and difficult to deal with. When this happens you may become seriously perplexed.

One interviewee who had lost his wife described his emotional state as having a pinball machine experience. (For those of you who don't know what a pinball machine is . . . well, you'll have to look it up!)

I can't figure out my emotional swings. I never know where the [emotional] ball is going to roll. It could bounce all over the place back and forth to the same emotional point several times, and miss other emotions entirely. The next event would be entirely different and I seem to have little control over the movement of the ball. My emotions could go all over the place. JA

Why did the stages seem to catch on; why did they become so popular? Perhaps the "stage theory fulfills a broader psychological need, the 'human desire to make sense of how the mind processes and may come to accept events and circumstances that it finds wholly unacceptable.'"[28] The mind resists disorder. For some, the stages seemed to offer a measure of order as they faced confusion and disorder.

There is another matter about which you should be aware. If you read a variety of literature to help you deal with your grief (called bibliotherapy, see chapter fifteen), you may become aware that writers differ in how they believe you should deal with your grief. A prevailing approach today is one that suggests that you understand that grief is something through which you must work. In this view, dealing with your grief is a matter of working at various tasks to move you through and beyond a particular aspect of grief. The goal of this approach is to resolve grief and to bring your life back to reasonable normalcy. Sometimes this process is called Reconciliation of Grief.[39] One counselor put it this way: "As a griever, you need to appreciate the fact that grief is work. It requires the expenditure of both physical and emotional energy. It is no less strenuous a task then digging a ditch or any other physical labor. The term 'grief work' was coined by psychiatrist Erich Lindemann in 1944 to describe the tasks and processes that you must complete successfully in order to resolve your grief. The term suggests that grief is something you must work at actively if you are to resolve it in a healthy fashion. It demands much more than merely passively experiencing your reactions to and action to integrate and resolve your grief."[40]

This perspective suggests that you should address your grief actively; that, "Grief is something you have to work at . . . The analogy that we use is if you broke your leg you wouldn't just sit there and do nothing."[41] "The prescription to tackle grief work may seem strange to you," say Zonnebelt-Smeenge and DeVries, "But if you're going to grieve anyway, why not work as hard as possible to help yourself?"[42]

Indeed, some advocates of the grief work approach suggest that if grief is not addressed properly there may very well be serious consequences. According to them, the worst thing a griever can do is resist, suppress or ignore grief. They are convinced that, "unmanifested grief will be found expressed to the full in some way or another."[43]

Perhaps that perspective has stimulated the growth of counseling centers, private and group therapy sessions, small griever support groups, grief websites, gatherings known as the Widowbago,[44] the proliferation of literature for the grieving and the rise of the grief industry. There is an assumed therapeutic value in the public expression of grief. It is assumed that a griever needs to work at or work through the grief process in order to realize optimum emotional recovery, but frankly, little is known about the benefit of such expression. Assumed as well is that reluctance to give outward expression to grief will bode negatively for the griever. "(T)he belief in grief work seems almost as intractable as the belief in a series of stage."[45]

There is however, an approach to grief that is essentially passive. After all, it is not natural to view one's loss as the onset of a major task or a series of tasks. Grief is not customarily understood as work; it is viewed as something that is experienced which will dissipate over time. It is exhausting (see chapters thirteen and fourteen) but it is viewed as something that happens to us or within us. I return to my statement about the uniqueness of grief. Each one of you will deal with it in your own way.

I have identified two extreme approaches to dealing with grief: "It all depends on you, so get to work," or "there's nothing you can do about it so just sit tight and suck it up." In keeping with the idea that your grief is as unique as you are, I have stated that there is no correct method or schedule of grieving. You are not faced with an either or choice. As you deal with your grief, you will move along the axes of private versus public, prescriptive versus passive, demonstrative versus more subtle. You may choose to "work through" something or not. It is well not to think that you must choose between two options for dealing with your grief. You may, as many others have, benefit from approaches that exist between them in the margins of those extremes.

The End of Grief

These approaches attest to the complexities of the human mind and the wisdom of the Creator. God doesn't have emotions as we do; he has attributes that are infinite in their perfections. In God, there is no contradiction or confusion as far as these attributes are concerned. Sometimes we must think of God in human terms; we speak of him as having human-like form: God's ears are attentive; God's eyes are on us; God's arm is strong to save us; or we speak of him as having human-like passions: he loves righteousness and hates wickedness; he is patient; kind; jealous; etc. God is all these perfectly and simultaneously. He does not change. When we are in emotional turmoil we may turn to God who is perfectly stable, reliable, and faithful. Since he has all knowledge, he knows perfectly what each person experiences in his or her uniqueness. You may appeal to him for comfort and peace and he will give them to you.

The prophet Isaiah described the One who was to come, who, as the Servant of the LORD would carry out Israel's commission and at the same time suffer for the transgression of God's people. Isaiah referred to that coming One as "a man of sorrows and acquainted with grief."[29] Sorrow and grief were part of Christ's experience. He was not spared that kind of mental anguish, but what is more, Isaiah went on to declare that the coming One would also bear the grief and carry the sorrows of God's people.[30] In the context of Isaiah's glorious fifty-third chapter, Isaiah linked the sorrow and grief of the Messiah to his being stricken by God for the transgression of God's people.[31] God placed the weight and the penalty for the iniquities of his people upon Christ. It was the will of the LORD to crush him; to put him to grief, making Christ's soul an offering for guilt.[32] Christ wept at the loss of his dear friend Lazarus;[33] he was touched by the sorrow of Lazarus' two sisters, Mary and Martha.[34] He was despised, rejected, misunderstood, and maligned. His teaching was twisted by his opponents; he was falsely accused. He wept over the hardness of heart of the residents of Jerusalem and because of the judgment that was coming upon them.[35] And, since he suffered being tempted, he is able to sympathized with us in our weaknesses.[36]

Grief began in the Garden of Eden with the entrance of sin; the cross signals its end. At the cross, God's justice for offenses against him was satisfied and his love for those hostile to him was illustrated supremely. God dealt with the root cause of all grief.

Because of what Christ accomplished at the cross, those who have faith in God through him look forward to when, "he will wipe every tear from their eyes and death shall be no more, neither shall there be mourning, nor crying, nor pain anymore, for the former things have passed away."[37]

What a joyful, amazing prospect for God's people! That prospect – among other wonderful benefits – was achieved for them at the cross. Until this future becomes the reality for God's people, we will groan and grieve over those whom we have lost to death, but not as those who have no hope.[38] Christ was the supreme sufferer. He is God's ultimate answer to our grief, and our hope is in him. With this as our perspective, even in our grief we may glorify God.

Chapter Thirteen

The Emotional Side

The heart knows its own bitterness; and no stranger knows its joy. (Proverbs 14:10)

Emotions are powerful. Sometimes during the sadness of caring for my wife in her last weeks, I wished I could have cried, a gut-wrenching, all-out cry, but the tear tank was empty. Perhaps having an all-out cry would have been a relief or would have served to dissipate some of the stress and sorrow. Some men can and do weep freely, but I can't. In the months closer to my wife's passing, my eyes would at times be filled with tears. Slowly tears would run down my face like warm salty streams. I'd wiped them away. Perhaps I should have allowed them to flow more freely and even welcomed their presence when they came. Several months after Grace's death, tears would sometimes well up in my eyes. What made that happen – a look at her picture, making a cup of tea; driving the car along a road we frequently traveled? For apparently no discernible reason, my eyes will fill with tears. I'd shake my head, purse my lips and go on, feeling deep sadness. The sadness put me on "pause". Then someone might ask a question or activities interrupt and require more attention than I was giving. I was jarred back into focus.

The men I interviewed reported that they experienced several emotions related to the loss of their wives, emotions that were common to all of them.

Isolation

The loss of your wife is manifested through your emotions. That emotional side of things includes loneliness, listlessness and lethargy. It takes in sadness, isolation, anger, the inability to concentrate, and dealing with one's identity without a wife. I want briefly to address some of these issues. I have learned from widower interviewees, my reading and my own status as a widower that isolation is a fact of life experienced by many who have lost their wives. "Social isolation and loneliness are demoralizing conditions. Some of us may crave attention more than others, but none of us thrive when left totally alone. Serious illness, caregiving and grieving are essentially lonely journeys."[1] If you had been your wife's caregiver, you understand that the role you played did not allow for you to engage in many social activities. You may have curtailed all socializing to attend to concerns associated with your wife's final illness. All during that time, your isolation was intentional and required. You made the right choice in providing care for your loved one in her decline. Doing so was part of the commitments you made in your wedding vows. Prior to her illness, much of your socializing was as a couple, but your wife's illness limited your social interactions. Isolation became necessary.

After the funeral your isolation probably continued. Isolation and loneliness feed on one another. Though people can and do feel lonely in a crowd, isolation accentuates the reality of loneliness. If you are isolated presently, there may be multiple reasons for it. Certainly one of the reasons involves the depression you could have felt after you lost your wife. You may have cared about very little at first, finding it difficult to generate a new interest in life. You probably were out of practice and even when you and your wife did socialize, she may have been the driver and organizer. In her absence you likely found that you were missing that significant social component. Now perhaps you just don't have it in you to ratchet up the interest in mingling again. Additionally, you may have felt awkward about resuming the social connections you shared with your wife because many of them were initially friends of your wife. "Social isolation is a depleting and demoralizing state of affairs."[2] A couple of the interviewees commented:

People respond to a couple as a couple; when one becomes single couples don't know how to respond. Friends drop away. I have no invitations at the present time. On the rare occasions that I would be invited to an event, I am by myself. I'm not a people person, so I often decline these kinds of invitations, but when I do accept them, I find myself isolated. I don't put myself out to be involved with other people. LL

Then too, you may want to avoid the inescapable questions about your well-being. They are sure to come. It's more comfortable for you not to face those encounters, as another interviewee suggested.

Shortly after [Heather died] I did not want fellowship. I think people knew it – that I just wanted to be left alone and that is what they did. ZB

Not facing those social situations may contribute to longer bouts with loneliness. It is more or less a tradeoff. If you chose the comfort of not facing awkward social situations, the result is isolation, which contributes to your loneliness. People were created as social beings. Social isolation for whatever reason is a condition contrary to a way we were meant to be. Another interviewee commented on his situation:

I know that isolating yourself is the worst thing you can do. I've talked with ... [widowers] who have told me that they have stayed at home for a whole year – just going to work and coming home. Another person told me [that] he went to work and just stayed home for six months and did nothing. AM

My wife and I would regularly visit with our good friends – another couple about our age. Sometime after my wife died, they really wondered if they should continue to get together as we had done before. We were no longer a foursome. Well, they continued to ask me over for dinner and other activities. I was glad they did. I know that they felt awkward, but I just needed that link. I didn't want to be cut off. I didn't necessarily need to talk about the loss of my wife; I just wanted to be able to talk with somebody about anything. I think widowers especially, need to have the social interaction. DM

Isolation is sometimes the consequence of people avoiding potentially awkward situations from their side. People don't know what to say or do, so they avoid the griever for fear of saying or doing something inappropriate: or of provoking an emotional response by the griever. Rather than to risk these things, they back away. A couple of the interviewees commented:

What I wish people would not do is avoid me when they know I'm in pain. I want them to be transparent, put their arms around me and tell me that they're praying for me. It seems that people avoid that. AM

When I attend some sort of party and I'm there by myself, [I'm] floating around. I'm not much of a talker anyway and so it was even more difficult. I would just pretty much sit there enjoying myself by myself watch[ing] everybody and [engage in] very shallow talk. So, that would be most awkward. I don't feel that I truly avoided any situation. If I went somewhere and it was awkward, and if I could leave, I would. RP

One estimate is that a grieving widow or widower may lose up to seventy-five percent of personal contact within the first year after the loss of a spouse.[3] Oates observes: "A considerable number of persons huddle around most people at the first moments and days of a crisis. But it does not take long for this crowd to thin out as they go back to work and resume the routine of life. This is when a shocked, numbed, depressed victim of crisis faces going back to work in a regular routine of life alone."[4] "What is clear is that it is likely that couples living without children in the home are more open to isolation after they lose their spouse."[5]

A Personal Note About Isolation:

I am introverted. I have very few close friends. My wife was also my best friend and she is gone. I had expressed my deepest and most private thoughts and hopes to her, but when she died there was no one to take her place. It takes time to build the kind of trust relationship that I needed then. When I moved from the area where my wife and I had lived for thirty years, I left a loose network of friends behind. In my new situation, people had their trust networks in place. Breaking into a new group seems easier than forming a new trusted network of go-to people. There has to be mutuality in these support networks and since I was new, I was not yet trusted sufficiently to be anyone's preferred go-to person and I did not feel comfortable to entrust myself to anyone. Consequently, there was no mutuality. Trusting and being trusted take time. Trust is developed. My need was immediate! That made things a little tougher! It was all part of the loneliness that is so very BIG right now!

I needed a close friend with whom I could speak freely, someone who could be trusted – I mean trusted with what I said and who would take it to the grave! To me it is of little value to have to be guarded in conversation, to talk only superficially about my deepest concerns at this point in my life situation. The easy, casual talk does no good in easing the ache in my heart. I don't feel I need a lot of advice right now, just someone who will honestly listen, who will not compromise confidences. I wanted the level of trust in a confidant that I would give to someone else in my situation. At present, I am thankful for one person who will from time to time ask me, "How is your spirit?" and by that means, "How are you holding up; how's your perspective; how has God supplied your needs?" The opportunity to speak frankly and without the concern of being judged if I happen to be down in spirit is a true blessing.

What a delight it would be to talk with someone and be as sure as is humanly possible that that person would not repeat our private exchanges, or judge the rightness or wrongness of my statements. How comforting it would be to relax and simply talk though troubles! We would not necessarily have to talk about my loss and grief; we could talk about anything, but nothing would be "off-the-table". This would be therapeutic to soften my loss and lighten my grief.

If you are grieving the loss of your wife, God is the one to whom you may safely go and to whom you may pour out your deepest sorrow. He is safe, trustworthy and kind. He will never get tired of listening to you. Nothing need be "off the table" with him. If you can talk with no one else, be assured that you can talk with God. He understands you perfectly and cares for you infinitely. Trust him!

Loneliness

There is another aspect to the emotional side of grief, one that is perhaps the most prevalent. I touched on it in my personal comment. Research in the area of grief after loss suggests that for both widows and widowers, "loneliness was their single greatest difficulty during the first two years of bereavement and that completing the tasks of daily living was their second most difficult problem."[6] We should note the difference between isolation and loneliness. Isolation may be described in terms of objective behaviors such as turning down invitations to "grab a bite to eat," or declining offers for visits or choosing to stay home. It is withdrawal from social interaction. Loneliness, on the other hand, is subjective; it is a feeling. Someone can be involved socially and yet feel lonely. By the same token, someone could be isolated but not lonely.[7]

Early in my pastoral ministry one of my predecessors returned to visit the area where he had ministered prior to my service there. He had retired and during that retirement had lost his wife. In our conversation about his situation his eyes filled with tears. He mentioned his wife and became silent. I asked if he were alright. He replied: "Oh, I'm just lonely I guess, very lonely. I can't get her out of my mind – not that I'd want to [long pause]... I'll be ok."

My wife and I used to visit a widowed friend. Before the death of her husband, we would socialize as couples. A few years after her husband died, I asked her what the greatest difficulty was for her in her adjustment as a widow. Not hesitating at all she replied, "Loneliness; loneliness is BIG!"

Without a doubt, loneliness ranks number one when it comes to identifying the greatest emotional challenge for widowers. Interviewees responded most freely when answering questions about loneliness. It is evident by the lengthy answers to the questions on this subject that loneliness dominated all other emotions the men said they experienced.

The hardest thing was all the loneliness and the quiet house which [was] accentuated
by going home every night after work and just being totally [alone]; no one to talk

to; just me and the four walls so to speak. That was really tough. I hated it! When I got to thinking about it, that was the first time in my entire life that I've ever lived alone . . . That was rough for me. DM

It was hard for me after Rhonda passed away; it was in two [areas], two dominant feelings of mine were loneliness and the other was [that] . . . after being the caretaker for so many years . . . I was exhausted! SJ

It's definitely lonely right from the start and the longer the time goes, the lonelier it is. I knew that I was the kind of person that did not want to be alone and I did not want to live alone. I just found that after a year or so I was just going everywhere alone coming home alone; and then after a while, I was not going anywhere. I wanted to go to some musical but I didn't want to go [alone] and so I didn't go and then that really bothered me after a while. I was doing the things that I wanted to do and couldn't seem to get it together alone . . . I thought that I would never be lonely because I had so many interests. I have so many different things I'd like to do that [I] always thought, "Well, even if I lost my spouse, I would be so busy keeping with everything that I wouldn't get lonely. [I] wouldn't miss [her]." That wasn't the case. It is true, you can be interested in all the activities you want to, but it still ... at night it's lonely and it's a different life than when you have someone. RP

Loneliness seems to arise more in the morning than in the afternoon. I have to get out of the house. I still have to structure my days and weeks ahead of time. I schedule what's coming up. So planning ahead helps me deal with loneliness. Just getting out of the house helps. I get out and go. I need to get out and just be with other people. I think that that helps loneliness. Also I learned that loneliness is time that you can really grow and learn things about yourself. AM

I am alone without Lindsey – all the things that she brought with her—infectious joy and personality [are gone]. She was the one who would make it easy in a social situation, because she could talk to anybody. She was the one that lit up the room. When she walked in [the room] she was the one who was focused on all the time. So I could take whatever part I was supposed to take in a social situation. I'm not lonely when I'm engrossed in something. I really enjoy my job and it's thoroughly engrossing for the most part. Now, that doesn't mean that, when I sit back and it's time for me to get up and take a break, that I don't think immediately of Lindsey . . .

I do not consciously have a strategy and I don't know how to make it [loneliness] go away. I can't do that. The only one thing I do, I pray; I plead with the Lord to calm me down. JA

Loneliness is not a slight emotional response to loss; it can be part of a physical dimension that must be addressed head-on. John Cacioppo, Director of the Center for Cognitive and Social Neuroscience at the University of Chicago has stated: "People who feel consistently lonely have a fourteen percent higher risk of premature death than those who don't . . . The impact of loneliness on early death is almost as strong as being poor, which increased the chances of dying early by nineteen percent . . . research found. Loneliness is a risk factor for early death beyond what can be explained by poor health behaviors."[8] If you are lonely, acknowledge it and tell someone. You should not be embarrassed about being lonely. People who know that you have lost your wife will understand and may be able better to help you.

Inability to Concentrate

These are thoughts captured in my journal after I moved into my condo. "I find it difficult to concentrate for any length of time. I'll sit at my desk to begin writing or reading and just mind-wander. I constantly have to pull myself back to the tasks I have assigned to myself. At other times, I find myself walking through the empty rooms of my house with my hands clasped behind me looking at the ceiling, trying to walk my way free of loneliness; I call it lacing and pacing. I have my routes, my loops through the rooms. My movement is a somber shuffle. I'm just moving, needing to move so as not to be still. Then I'll fold my arms across my chest or put my hands in my pockets and walk and walk some more. Though that activity is not deliberate, in some ways, through it, I seem to be able to spend built-up energy! I look at the empty rooms, the pictures, plaques, knickknacks and vases – all silent and waiting for some indication of activity! I will continue to walk, looking at the ceiling only to have it stare back at me in silence. I walk upstairs for . . . well, I don't know, but the upstairs rooms provide just as convenient a pacing turf as the level below. I'll meander in a circle or follow the design of the room. It doesn't matter. Perhaps I'm trying to walk away from my loneliness. At times I'll sit to ponder – whatever comes into my mind – until I decide that I'm not making good use of time and go to try perform another chore."

Why is this so? Kelly speaks of the difficulty in concentrating after losing someone close to you: "Most of us have some difficulty concentrating or remembering when we are grieving. Perhaps you will have bursts of energy and start a project, either at home or at work, and then find that the energy is short-lived and that you cannot concentrate on the project or cannot even remember what it is you're supposed to be doing. For many of us, making decisions becomes difficult or even impossible. This doesn't just apply to big decisions – I think most of us can understand why conventional wisdom advises those who are grieving not [to] make major decisions at first. But even little, everyday decisions – what to wear, what to eat, the process of getting up and going to work – can be difficult too."[9]

Why can't those who are grieving and who are aware of the mind's tendency to drift off compensate and concentrate? Amit Sood suggests that the mind has two working modes, focus and default. In the focus mode, the brain is stimulated by external stimuli that perceive the world as an object of attention, as interesting, meaningful, and exciting. It is outward directed. When attention is directed inwardly, the mind is likely to operate in default mode. Our brains are constantly active. They do not rest. If they are not directed to specific task oriented goals, they default to consolidating previous thoughts and experiences. The brain is always ready to spring back into focus mode when and if needed, but the default mode of the mind wanders, "weaves stories together, imagines what-ifs and spins directionless dialogue, pulling in superficially related facts from different time periods."[10] Sood attests that the unhappy mind spends more time in default mode. "A ruminating mind – a mind repeating thoughts about the past – is predisposed to depression. It becomes more difficult for the depressed brain to suppress its default mode."[11]

Our brains are inundated with numerous decisions each day. Sometimes they are overwhelmed with the welter of multiple thoughts. Essentially, there are a lot of open files that our brains are processing. Perhaps this is analogous to a computer running several programs simultaneously. The processor can handle just so much and when you ask your computer to perform another function, it is sluggish and you wait and wait until previous tasks are sufficiently completed. In your grieving, your mind is dealing with many "open files" and running several programs. No wonder it is sluggish. Unless you can focus your mind's attention on something external to get out of the default mode, you will find it difficult to concentrate. This experience may also contribute toward making you lethargic. You don't feel like doing much of anything that requires initiative. You may become indifferent to your own needs; you may recognize that certain chores need to be done but you just don't care. This is part of what you will likely experience as you grieve the loss of your wife. There will be a few suggestions in the next chapter to help you address the difficulties in concentrating and in dealing with isolation, loneliness and lethargy.

Days and Dates

Emotions come to bear especially on holidays and days that were memorable for you and your wife. The first Thanksgiving Day celebration without my wife went well. My daughter had invited several guests and in the past, my wife and I had often been part of those festivities. Of course, we could not be present the final year of my wife's illness. Frankly, I was surprised at how "normal" the celebration went [and I think that others were too]! I was engaged in the table conversation and the activities that followed. Still, it was a lonely time at my new home afterwards.

When the first Christmas without my wife came, I had to remember that my children and other members of the family would experience their first holiday season without their mother as well! The grandchildren would not have grandma to given them attention and affection. That first Christmas was no small concern. How would I, how would we manage? Christmases have always been times of family gathering, reminiscing and recalling the past, a time of story-telling and remembering past Christmases. My wife and I had tried our best to be with our children during the Christmas and New Year's Day holidays – even though doing so sometimes involved travel in opposite directions from where we lived in order to be with our children in different parts of the country. We would split our time. Sometimes family members would travel in our direction.

That first Christmas after my wife's passing, I wanted to be with my family. I didn't want to be alone. My thoughts were that if I could get the rest of the family to travel to my location, we could be together. I had plenty of room in my condo to bed and board my other children and grandchildren, so, I invited them to come for a visit during the Christmas holiday. My younger son flew in from the Carolinas and my older son with his family drove in from Minnesota. We were all together. I think everyone wanted to be together that first Christmas without mom – if only to support dad. Again, the busyness of preparation for hosting everyone kept my mind from wandering into loneliness. It was therapeutic preparation. I had come up with a loose agenda of activities that would appeal to older and younger alike – a mix of indoor and outdoor activities. The plan worked well and there was more than enough to do to keep everyone occupied.

I knew that there would probably be a let-down after everyone left, so I planned a New Year's Eve get-together with new friends. The planning for this coincided with the planning for Christmas. You might wonder why I would want to undertake such a gathering so soon after Christmas events. I can say only that it was something I felt I had to do. My wife and I had always spent New Year's Eve together. In her absence, I would be alone. Seventeen people were asked to come to my place for a low-key New Year's Eve gathering; twelve of them were able to come. Each brought a little something to eat. There was no agenda. This would be a time to relax and enjoy one another's company. It had been over ten years since my wife and I had attempted something along these lines. I was apprehensive, but I felt I had to do it! The last of my children and grandchildren left on New Year's Eve morning and I promptly went about readying the condo for that evening. To my surprise and delight, all went well. The guests started the conversations going; there were plenty of refreshments. The party carried itself.

I say all this to remind you and myself that in spite of the loss of a loved one and probably because of the loss of a loved one, one needs to stay involved in the stream of life. To withdraw or isolate oneself would be counterproductive and most likely harmful. Engaging in these social activities isn't pretending that the loss didn't take place or that it wasn't as devastating as it was. It is a simple matter of realizing that life goes on with or without you. Waiting for just the right feeling to get involved again is not the best approach to dealing with grief. That "right feeling" may be long in coming and may never come at all. Resume what for you was a normal course of life as soon as you can. Some of the interviewees related some of the challenges they face socially after the death of their wives.

The people I know really think that you're not the same person. Your wife kind of makes up half of you socially. How they react to you is not as the same person you were [when you socialized along with your wife]. I never had a lot of guy friends, really. So it's hard for those friends of mine [who were our friends] to know how to react in an awkward situation. I don't feel comfortable interacting with them as much. I feel that they ask, "Do we invite him for doing A and B?" It seems difficult for them to address. SJ

My wife and I would regularly visit with our good friends – another couple about our age. Sometimes after my wife died, they really wondered if we should continue to get together as we had done before. We were not longer a foursome. Well, we continued to ask me over for dinner and other activities. I was glad they did. I know that they felt awkward, but I just needed that link. I didn't want to be cut off. I didn't necessarily need to talk about the loss of my wife; I just wanted to be able to with somebody about anything. I think widowers especially, need to have the social interaction. DM

When I attend some sort of party and I'm there by myself [I'm] floating around. I'm not much of a talker anyway and so it was even more difficult. I would just pretty much sit there enjoying myself by myself watch[ing] everybody and [engage in] very shallow talk. So that would be most awkward. I don't feel that I truly avoided any situation. If I went somewhere and it was awkward, and if I could leave I would. RP

I'm not in the situations very often [where] I would never want people to just regard me with nothing but pity. I think that you know the understanding that I lost Lindsey has affected me. Don't treat me differently really, but when you invite me to things, you got to invite [me] with the understanding that I am not a couple. So don't invite me to things where everybody else is a couple; I can't participate in things [as a couple] because my other half isn't here. It can get really awkward in a hurry but for the most, [people] accept me for who I am and go forward. They don't have to talk about [my situation] a lot and I don't have to talk about it with them necessarily . . . I wouldn't want people to somehow treat me differently with a pair of kid gloves. In a way, just understand that I'm alone and so you can't expect me to interact as couple. JA

On the rare occasions that I would be invited to an event, I am by myself. I'm not a people person, so I often decline these kinds of invitations, but when I do accept them, I find myself isolated. I don't put myself out to be involved with other people. LL

Lethargy

I have included lethargy as a distinct symptom of the grief of loss. It in fact is part of a complex of emotions/conditions that may characterize grief. You might describe what you feel as being lazy or sluggish. It is a general feeling of indifference and weariness. Things that interested you, for the time, have ceased to interest you; you no longer, for the time, care about what was important to you. It is as though you have lost interest in life itself. It is a "not caring". Of course, down deep you care, but you are in such an emotional state that you do not want to do anything. You say to yourself: "The house needs decluttering; it can wait. The dirty dishes fill the sink. I'll get to it later! I see the dust covering the furniture. It's not hurting anything. The yard needs tending. I don't care. The bathrooms need cleaning. I don't feel like doing it."

When you are grieving, there are times your mind seems locked on one thing or on everything or on nothing at all. In any case, you can't think creatively or critically; your mind is in mental paralysis. You sit in silence, in wordless grief. Your body is tired and you feel like doing absolutely nothing. That is what you do – nothing. You feel a little worse because things are piling up. You know you should get after the chores but you don't have the energy or the will to start doing them. You're lethargic and if you are lonely and isolated, your condition seems (is) worse.

If you have lost your wife you will probably experience times of lethargy. You have been through significant stress. You may have gone through months of serious strain without taking a break. Taking a break would not have been possible as you were caring for your wife. Your heart is broken and you are physically exhausted. Your mind is filled with myriad thoughts and the total "you" wants to shut down. It's not surprising that you are lethargic. Some men deal with the complex of their emotions due to grief by talking to a few select friends; others may seek group counseling; most men, however, will distract themselves through activity. It is not as is frequently and popularly assumed, that dealing with grief through distraction is failure to face reality. Your mind is working all the time and it, by the grace and the power of God, will sort through all the issues you face. Little by little you will get better.

Our emotions are God-given; they are not something of which we should be ashamed or which we should hide. They are part of us and to a great extent make us who we are. We may not ever realize the intensity of our emotions until or unless we are overwhelmed by a life-shaking event like the death of a dear wife. We should give expression to our emotions, but society and personal history will weigh heavily on how we express them. Nevertheless, it is important to express them. You may feel that expressions of your emotions are out of control. You are a unique individual and there are no standards for the proper expression of your emotions. There is always the danger of becoming obsessed, of just thinking about them too much. As a man you might feel that you have to get them under control. After a time, you will realize more composure, but by all means, don't suppress them. Your adjustment to your loss will take place slowly, but will never be complete in this life.

Chapter Fourteen

The Physical Side

My heart is broken within me; all my bones shake. (Jeremiah 23:9)

The physical and emotional sides of grief are not two unrelated aspects of experiencing loss. They are intimately related; they affect each other. If you provided care for your wife during her last illness, what is taking place in your life is affecting you in many ways; among them is what goes on with you physically. In the last chapter several emotional responses to loss were mentioned. You do not need to examine the results of a long and involved research study to convince you that mind and body work together.

Fatigue

If you are your wife's caregiver, you have already experienced loss which has taken a toll on you emotionally. You have experienced extraordinary stress over several weeks. The declining condition of your wife placed enormous demands upon you, and when you were exhausted, you continued to do what you needed to do in order to attend to the needs of your wife. It didn't matter that you were tired or really didn't feel like doing what needed doing. You did what was required just the same and pushed yourself to the limits. Perhaps you were not able to eat regularly to keep up your strength; or to sleep soundly and sufficiently to wake up refreshed.

I stayed with my wife during her last hospitalizations. Providentially, the hospital Grace and I chose to use was less than a mile from our home. Unlike many who must travel long distances to be with their wives during hospitalization, I was able to return home each night. Just the same, I was with my wife from twelve to sixteen hours a day. In the hospital, I would grab a piece of fruit from the snack shop or get a quick carry-back lunch from the cafeteria. When I did eat at home, it was late in the evening and usually from an assortment of prepared meals.

When Grace was discharged for the last time, she came home and into hospice care. I became her primary caregiver. At that point in her life she could eat only soft foods and very little of them. Much of her intake was soup or broth. I found that I too was eating less; I did not take the time to prepare individual, well-balanced meals for myself. Over the last year of Grace's life I lost about forty pounds – roughly the same amount of weight my wife lost! I didn't even know it was happening. I didn't realize my weight loss until after her death. A year later I had a physical exam and was startled at how much I had lost.

Additionally, my sleeping became less frequent and broken. My wife and I had to have separate sleeping arrangements. I learned that this is not unusual for couples who go through the final sickness of one of them. I missed her being beside me. I would place a large pillow behind me as I lay in bed to give me some sense of a physical presence. This practice was short-lived however. I became more accustomed to sleeping alone. Still, I remember the comfort of resting in bed together – not just the physical comfort but the psychological comfort as well. One may realize loneliness in many ways. During her hospice, I could sleep about fifteen feet away from my wife's bed but I subconsciously stayed alert to meet any need she might have. Again, I didn't realize at the time how physically taxing this entire experience was, but such is common. Reiss notes that: "Some family caregivers will reach the point of total exhaustion. Some will become depressed, anxious, irritable, or angry all the time. Others will start to experience weight loss or some other potential sign of ill health. Many will struggle with insomnia."[1] As a husband, you have the obligation to see to the needs of your wife, not just at the time of her last illness but especially then. Your attention naturally will be drawn to the care that you must provide – her physical, medical, emotional, and spiritual requirements. You may likely become so busy meeting your loved one's needs that you neglect your own well-being. The care your wife requires may be complex and cumbersome, but you give it. You are rightly concerned for your wife – her diet, medications, physical comforts, taking her for routine checkups and tests, but you may also dismiss any thoughts about your own health. The daily tasks of maintaining a home, possibly looking after your child(ren) and possibly attending to your employment arrangements do not stop. You (will) have little time for looking after yourself. It is well to remember that you can take good care of your loved one only as you remain physically healthy yourself.

As a widower, you are affected emotionally and physically to have physical responses to your wife's death. After the stress of having seen your wife's decline; after the physical weariness of having taken care of her, or attending to her being cared for; after the duress of making arrangements for the funeral and the funeral itself, you were physically and emotionally exhausted.

The experience of exhaustion after the passing of one's wife is not unusual. Some of the men I interviewed expressed their weariness in terms of exhaustion:

It was hard for me after Rhonda passed away . . . After being the caregiver for so many years it takes a toll on you physically and emotionally. I was exhausted! SJ

Before and after Carol went into hospice it was kind of like, well "I know what's going to happen". I was exhausted, so I did go home some nights when she was in hospice. RP

I was totally exhausted; I had been ill myself during the last months of my wife's illness and death. I was just numb at the time. I was living with my own pain at the time. I just told myself that I have to keep going. I think it was two weeks before I could feel anything. I told myself that I just have to keep going. Two weeks after the funeral I was so hit by what had happened that I felt crushed. I nearly collapsed. It really hit me. LL

Among the things you may expect after you have laid your wife to rest is that the physical weariness does not dissipate quickly. Your mind will continue to grieve. It is trying to adjust to the loss. Matters are unsettled in your thinking and will remain that way for some time. Your body will take its cues from your mind. Judith Heath avers that among the physical symptoms of grief are low energy or fatigue.[2] Grieving produces a weariness in every sense as exhausting as physical work. Grieving will wear you out; it will drain your energy and you may wonder why you continue to be so tired and sluggish most of the time. You may not have the energy to begin the smallest task. What's more, losing your wife drastically affects your sleep. Research has shown that "suffering from grief makes it harder to get enough hours of quality sleep."[3]

Sleep and Sleep loss

Some grievers go to bed early, sleep through the night, awake late in the morning and are tired enough to take naps throughout the day. They looked tired and they are tired. Others can't sleep; they go to bed late, rise early and stay busy throughout the day though they may get only two or three hours of sleep per night. I put myself in the second category. I felt tired but not sleepy. I would go to bed between midnight and one a.m., would lie awake for a couple of hours trying to relax but couldn't. I would look at the clock, sleep for what I thought was longer only to realize that I had slept for a little over an hour. For three years after my wife died I got about three hours of sleep per night. I did not take day naps. What Heath noted is true: "Most people in grief do not sleep well for long periods of time."[4]

Moreover, your own physical health might be at risk after the loss of your wife. Those who have given prolonged care to the terminally ill seem more susceptible to becoming ill themselves. "Grief can affect the immune system, and when you are grieving you are more likely to become sick. You may find you catch colds more easily or have recurrences of chronic condition such as back pain or depression."[5] "Suddenly bereaved persons are at risk for accidents, illnesses, or even death. Their immunological systems break down. Even cancer itself is thought to be related to such failures of the immunological system."[6] Widowhood appears to increase the risk of dying from almost all causes, including "cancer . . . The death of a spouse, for whatever reason, is a significant threat to health and poses a substantial risk of death by whatever cause."[7] It is ranked as the number one stressor. Another study shows that sixty percent of those who lose a spouse . . . "will *experience a serious illness* in the twelve months following that loss."[8] And, what is more, research "reveals that in the first six months of the loss of a spouse widows and widowers had a 41% higher risk of mortality."[9]

God's word informs us that he knows every one of your days,[10] and that you cannot add a single hour to the length of your life by worrying.[11] In fact, worry and stress can shorten your life. You can die from a broken heart. Excessive loneliness for a spouse may bring on the pre-mature death of the survivor. Dr. Scott Sharkey, a cardiologist with the Minneapolis Heart Institute at Abbott Northwestern Hospital, affirms that people can die from a broken heart. "Doctors even have a not-so-subtle name for it: broken heart syndrome. 'Any cardiologist in town will tell you that they've seen several cases of this,' Sharkey said. He studies the medical condition, which is triggered by sudden, major stress. The symptoms are similar to a heart attack: shortness of breath, chest pains, and accelerated heartbeat. For senior citizens, this type of sudden heart injury can be especially dangerous when combined with pre-existing conditions and their age."[12] Be cautioned about the possible consequences of neglecting your own health after your wife has died. There is an emotional numbness that follows the loss of a spouse. A kind of apathy may affect you in ways that make you not want to care about anything (See previous chapter). Motivation to do much of anything is largely missing and one danger you face is in not taking care of yourself.

Do not be surprised if you notice *other* physical reactions to the loss of your wife. Among them have been identified dizziness, hair loss, shakiness or tremors, digestive difficulties, headaches. Take steps to promote your own health at this very critical time in your life![13]

The Place Of Work

I mentioned that I had purchased a condo that needed significant remodeling. Two months after my wife's death, I began the work; ripping up carpet and fixing the plumbing, demolishing old cabinetry, painting and plastering. In my mind, I had a sense of sequence to the overall project. I worked at remodeling and repair throughout the summer months as diligently as if I had been going to a place of employment each day. I *had* to be busy, I had to decompress slowly. The work was therapy; it effectively took my mind away from the sorrow of the last years. It made me think about something besides what I had been through. In this way I could process the experience of my wife's decline and death in my own way and at my own pace. The evenings would find me at my daughter's home for supper after which I would retire to my room where I read light novels. The next day the routine would be the same.

I realize that work may be seen as a way of escape – not dealing with reality. I suppose for some it is. Work can be seen as a distraction from pain. Men seem to throw themselves into work soon after the passing of their wives. Heath observes: "Many studies have been devoted to the differences between the sexes when it comes to grief. There are general differences. Women tend to cry more and have a need to talk about their losses. Men often clammed up and throw themselves into their work."[14] Some of the interviewees expressed their felt need to return to work soon after the death of their wives:

Some people really misunderstood my affections for Marla because I think it just took ... some of them completely by surprise. She passed away on Tuesday. We had a funeral that following Saturday and I was back in to work the following Monday morning. Some people just couldn't understand how I could be so callous going right back to work. DM

I went right back to work after three days of bereavement leave. I really had to get back to work since I had been away from my job taking care of Lindsey. Financially, I had to keep the money flowing. It has been a real blessing for me to be able to continue to work. I really enjoy my job and it's thoroughly engrossing for the most part. Now that doesn't mean that, you know, when I sit back and it's time for me to take a break, that I don't think immediately of Lindsey. JA

I tried to kill my loneliness with activities. I have to keep busy. ZB

I just keep busy with my job and activities. That was my way of handling my loneliness. After Sherri's death, I was back to work within a week. EF

It was good for me to continue to meet my work commitments. I gave my mind to work, so I didn't focus on my sorrow. LL

I'm here [alone] and I can remember waiting for the weekend to be over so I could to back to work to be around people. AM

This is not unusual. "The bereaved may . . . hasten back into hyperactive work, almost as if nothing has happened. Grief . . . may be delayed over a long period of time."[15]

In the past, I have usually been able to deal with stress about most anything through physical work. I know that is true for me. After Grace' death, physical work distracted me from my thinking and delayed my dealing with my loss. Working wasn't avoidance; it simply allowed me to parse out my grief in manageable portions and to address it on my own terms. If I had not been retired at the time of my wife's death and still working, I believe it would have been counterproductive to take an extended bereavement leave in order to grieve. If you have recently lost your wife, it may not help you to sit for long periods of time and to reflect on what happened to you. Get out of the house and do something physical. Take walks, paint a room, repair a broken window, or take care of the yard. You will not be able to grieve in a hurry. Take the time deliberately to do something physical. It may be that you golf or ride a bicycle or hike or go to the gym as an activity. Your physical activity can help your mind heal and allow you better to cope with your loss.

The physical manifestations of grief are too numerous to discuss here, but they relate to what is taking place in your mind and heart. Pay attention to the physical and emotional effects of your grief. Don't be surprised by conditions you had not experienced previously. Perhaps they are related to the stress of your loss and a part of your grief. Don't deny these conditions or feelings. You could create misunderstandings among your friends and family members; you could complicate your recovery. Don't dismiss them as "nothing" or as something that you can handle. You are human, after all and subject to all the frailties and conditions of humanity.

Chapter Fifteen

Recovery And Closure

He will wipe away every tear from their eyes, and death shall be no more, neither shall there be mourning, nor crying, nor pain anymore, for the former things have passed away. (Revelation 21:4)

You have experienced what may be considered the greatest loss of your life. Life for you has changed and will continue to change. Change is constant. We understand that intellectually, yet there are times in our lives when change seems more obvious. There are seasons of transition throughout life and you have entered into some of those seasons of dramatic change. Newly married couples experience life together; there must be adjustment. That requires change. Children coming into the picture, job relocations, needs of a growing family – these all require change. We pass certain milestones through life and each one marks some kind of change. As change takes place, *you* change. God is the only one who does not change.[1] All your experiences contribute to making you who you are.

Presently, you are experiencing emotional pain; you are grieving the loss of your wife. You may very well wonder, "When does the pain go away?" You can be sure that your pain and sorrow will diminish over time. Resumption of your activities or engaging in new ones will reduce your sorrow; establishing new relationships will serve in the same way. Nevertheless, you will continue to live with your loss until you die. Will you get "closure" on this loss?

Closure – does it exist when it comes to coping with the loss of a loved one? Is the term appropriate for describing part of the grieving a person does? Is closure a goal to be attained when grieving the death of your wife? I venture a qualified "No" to all of the above. It is perhaps better to think in terms of progress you have made in adjusting to your loss. No one "gets over" the loss of a wife, but life itself is constant change and accommodation to change. The wife you married ten, twenty, thirty, forty or more years ago influenced you immeasurably. Your lives were woven together like a tapestry. You will never be able to discount that influence. Moody and Arcangel remind us that use of the term *closure* came out of the medical profession. They use the analogy of doctors treating an open wound. Doctors gather the materials they need to make repairs and close the affected area as soon as they can. Such treatment promotes healing and protects the heathy cells. It is initiated at the *beginning* of a healing process. "Grief counselors adopted the term closure from the medical profession and initially it was an effective metaphor. When the deep wound of a loss occurs, the psyche needs protection from further injury, the gathering of loose ends and precious time for rebuilding.[2] Popularly however, closure has come to be used as the *ending* of an adjustment or healing process rather than to describe the onset of that process. The term is inappropriate. In her presentation of the stages of death and dying, Kübler-Ross identified *acceptance* as the last stage, but to be sure, there are those who resist death until their last breath; they never accept it. You will never forget your loved one; she will always have a place in your heart and mind. "You may hear the word 'closure' associated with acceptance, but people in grief, especially grief due to tragic loss, often considered [sic] this [term as] terribly overrated and carelessly used. The reason is that [y]our grief is caused not by the presence of something, but by its absence. Nothing can bring back that which [is] desperately desire[d] for real closure to exist."[3]

The following article on closure was taken from the Journeys Newsletter, February, 1999 produced by the Hospice Foundation of America.[4]

When will I begin to feel better? When will I return to normal? When will I achieve some closure?" grievers often ask. Closure, our culture tells us, will bring about a tidy ending, a sense of completion. Some grievers hope that the desired magical closure will occur after the funeral or memorial service. Others are confident it will come once they have cleared out their loved one's room. Or maybe after a special personal ritual. Or perhaps after the first anniversary comes and goes. "Surely then, we will have some closure," we think. We pray.

The reason we long for closure, of course, is because we would like to neatly seal away all of this pain. We would like to close all of the sad, confused, desperate, angry feelings out of our life. We would like to put all of this behind us.

Closure. What an odd concept really, as if we could truly close the door on pain, turn the lock and throw away the key. The truth is far more complex, of course.

Closure is for business deals. Closure is for real estate transactions. Closure is not for feelings or for people we love.

Closure simply does not exist emotionally, not in a pure sense. We cannot close the door on the past as if it didn't exist because after losing someone dear to us, we never forget that person or the love we shared. And in some ways, we never entirely get over the loss. We learn to live with the loss, to integrate it into our new identity.

Imagine if we really could end this chapter in our life, completely, it would mean losing our memories, our connections to those we love. If we really found closure, it would ironically hurt even more because the attachment would be severed. And this attachment is vital to us, the memories are treasures to be held close, not closed out.

Perhaps it is better to think in terms of healing. Yes, we can progress our pain and move to deeper and deeper levels of healing. Yes, we can find ways to move on and channel our pain into productive activities. Yes, we can even learn to smile again and laugh again and love again.

But let's not ever think that we'll close the door completely on what this loss means, for if we did that, we would unwittingly close the door on all the love that we shared. And that truly would be a loss too terrible to bear."

"Closure" is a word, "which ... many ... survivors detest. There is no closure ... People will insist we have closure, because they think it will be better for you and for them. It is crucial to remember that this is your grief and it will take as long as it needs. There is no way to will 'getting over' these things."[5] In fact, "Closure does not solve grief. Grief can't be managed with closure."[6] In reality, grievers achieve *sufficient* acceptance and understanding of their loss to permit resumption of a mostly forward-looking life.

As the scripture cited above indicates, there is a time of real closure. It is not in this life, however. Look at it once again. It refers to a time when there will no longer be any cause for sorrow or grief. "He will wipe away every tear from their eyes, and death shall be no more, neither shall there be mourning, nor crying, nor pain anymore, for the former things have passed away." The "he" of course is God. God will remove all pain, heartache and suffering; he will remove whatever causes pain – physical, mental and spiritual. The scene the passage describes is the New Heavens and the New Earth. Sin and corruption will be banished; nothing will remain of the old age that brings tragedy, trial, or trouble. The terrors of the former life will not come to mind. In this life all will suffer and all will die, but God will redeem his own people and they will be his people forever and he will be their God. During this life is the only time we can get prepared for the next.

Are you prepared? As long as your life may be, it is but a single drop in the ocean of eternity. What better time than now to turn to God in your grief?

Chapter Sixteen

What You Can Do

"I perceived that there is nothing better than to be joyful . . . and that everyone should eat and drink and take pleasure in all his toil – this is God's gift to man (Ecclesiastes 3:12-13)."

God has created human beings with an immense capacity for learning new things; he implanted a desire and a need for growth. We have been given potential that we have not explored, abilities which we have not touched. To be sure, we are limited by our finitude, but remember, we are image-bearers of the Creator, with whom there is infinite variety. Every one of us has been given talent, skills, insights, and abilities that we can develop, and we please God when we do develop them. There are interests that each person may pursue for his or her enjoyment and betterment. Pursuing these may also be helpful in coping with loss – not merely as diversions or distractions, but as worthwhile activities in themselves. Everyone reading this has been involved in arts and crafts or music, participated in sports or used skills for his or her own enjoyment. Involvement in these or other activities should continue after the loss of your loved one.

Creativity

If you have a skill – a hobby or a craft – that you enjoyed before your wife died, continue to practice that skill. Doing something with your hands that occupies your mind is therapeutic. It directs your thoughts and energies on a specific project while at the same time reduces your focus on your own condition. Sometimes this kind of activity is referred to as expressive therapy.

Twenty-five years before my wife died, I had taken up the hobby of cutting stained glass. I started doing smaller projects that required four or five cut pieces of glass, and progressed to stain glass lampshades and smaller stain glass light-catchers. Eventually, I received a request and a commission to make a commemorative window for a local church. Later, due to relocation and a couple of moves, I put a hold on my hobby. About six years ago, I took it up again when I was asked to create a large circular window for someone's home. I agreed to do it. It was a challenge and required concentrated thought, imagination, problem solving skills and the use of my hands. When the project was completed and installed, it gave me personal satisfaction as well as delighted the homeowner. You cannot allow your attention to drift too far when you focus on the details of a particular project – especially when it is cutting glass. You engage your mind and body in creation. I have done two smaller projects since my wife passed away. Creating something – using imagination and skills to bring it about – is wonderful therapy. It gets one's mind off self and directs it outward.

"Everyone possesses the ability to create something useful for self or others. You already have that creative energy within . . . Write a book, a blog, or an article about the lessons you have learned from your experience. What are the tangible takeaways from what you are going through? There are many. If you are skilled with your hands, build something, draw, or paint a picture ... Never confuse creating something with keeping busy. Creating with intention will energize you, if you limit doubt or disbelief from blocking your path. By the same token, creating provides an uplifting spiritual boost."[1]

Reading

Perhaps you can realize some relief from your grief through reading. Some of the men interviewed said that they turned to literature on grief and the loss of loved ones to find direction. They wanted to understand what had taken place in their lives—reading not so much for comfort but for information. One of the interviewees commented:

I started reading books about grief and got familiar with it because I didn't really understand. I knew what my Christianity said, but I [also] knew I didn't really understand my grief ... I wanted to understand ... about her death and why it happened and all that. That's why I thought it wise to read all the books [I could] and try to understand the whole thing. My greatest comfort was learning, reading and understanding what the Bible says about what happened to me and finding God's purpose in what happened to me; in improving me as a Christian with greater understanding and belief. RP

During the interviewing process, this man admitted to bewilderment and confusion about what had happened to him. He wanted answers. Another said:

I carry a book with me wherever I go . . . I find that reading brings a lot of healing too. So those are my ways of dealing with loneliness. AM

Grief counselors refer to his approach to grief as bibliotherapy. "Bibliotherapeutic techniques or reading self-help literature may also be highly effective with masculine grievers. Bibliotherapy, in general, has been found to be a useful resource for the bereaved."[2] Researcher Dale Lund states that the "fact that [bibliotherapy] is active, cognitive, self-regulated and solitary in nature may make it especially well-suited to some of the masculine grieving style."[3] He notes that "rather than externalize their grief, many men choose to confront their losses internally. Men are more comfortable in dealing with grief cognitively."[4] Men seem to want to think about their loss rather than to tell you how they are feeling about it.

Writing Therapy

Writing is beneficial as well. I did not intend to write a book after my wife passed away; I did not keep a journal prior to Grace's death. It was only as I needed some kind of relief, a way to express my thoughts some weeks after I relocated, that I began to jot down random thoughts. It gave me a measure of satisfaction to begin to sort the jumbled thoughts in my mind. It was as though I could say, "That series of events is in order; that thought has been recorded." It was as though I didn't need to think about that thought again. I'm convinced that journaling provided emotional benefits that I had not been able to realize in another way.

Journaling has been shown to be beneficial for those who are experiencing grief. Psychologist Dr. Kriss Wiant points to studies on the psychological profit of writing down one's thoughts, if for no other reason than to sort through them and isolate them for reflection. He attests to the therapeutic value of journaling.[5] There are several advantages to writing: "Putting your thoughts and feelings on paper is a catharsis recommended by psychologists and psychiatrists worldwide for a variety of emotional ills and to better understand your inner world. The consistent use of writing is one of the most effective and least used ways to manage the pain of grief. It will help you physiologically, especially in your immune system, as well as emotionally, according to Dr. James Pennebaker of the University of Texas at Austin. Allowing feelings created by your thoughts to flow from your head, down through your hand, and on to paper is a releasing process in itself."[6]

Keeping a journal during the weeks and months after the loss of your wife may help you think through your thoughts and feelings about death. Jenkins advises: "Take your journal with you everywhere you go and use it as an outlet for your emotions. Many people write about how they react to events of the day. Many write poetry, even if they have never written poetry before. Some write deeply personal things or things they want to say to their loved one. Some write things they want to share later with others."[7]

What's more, your record will preserve important information for later review and reflection. Not only will you record your feelings, but you will also record the details of the events surrounding your wife's passing. You may have already forgotten some of the Who's, What's, When's and Where's of the last weeks with your wife. As long as you live you will not forget the loss of your wife, but some of the details and sequencing of events may become obscure. Also, friends and extended family may want to understand what both you and your wife went through. Certainly, not everyone will want or need the total story, but writing will help you refine your thoughts and enable you to create both shorter and longer versions of your story.

Music and Music Therapy

Dr. Dale Taylor suggests that "Musical perception and participation stimulate the brain to organize incoming stimuli and to plan and execute corresponding behavior, thereby enhancing perceptual ability, cognitive processing, and interactive response capacity."[8] In other words, being involved in music helps you heal.

Studies have been conducted on the pharmacological benefits of music therapy once traditional drug support is no longer working.[9] Important chemicals such as adrenalin, norepinephrine, dopamine and serotonin are produced in the brain when music is heard.[10] Listening to music has been shown to stimulate the nervous system to produce new synaptic pathways,[11] as well as increasing the availability of the brain's chemical messengers.

Hearing music can calm the living and the dying, but it also has a restorative effect on the depressed and distressed. Taylor has demonstrated that, "music positively affects people's moods, and that the degree of familiarity with the music may affect the degree of mood response. ... [Those] who like music are more likely to express a positive increase in mood, while subjects who do not like music are more likely to experience a mood decrease."[12]

Sometimes a person who is experiencing an emotional low needs, "to hear a sad song to work through [his] depression,"[13] Antes comments. She added that those who are grieving should not be so self-critical about what they may be feeling. "If you can't put what you are feeling into words, there may be another way for you to express your grief and process your feelings through music."[14] Those sad words may give expression to the very thoughts on the mind of the bereaved. "Grieving is enabled through music therapy".[15]

Words of a song may provide vocabulary to describe your experience. In yourself, you may not be able to find words to express what you feel, but you may discover them in a song. Relating to song lyrics appears to serve as affirmations that something of what you are experiencing is shared by others. The combination of words and music may speak to you in ways that mere prose cannot. You may be able to identify with the message of the music and to sort through the confusion brought about through the loss of your wife. Music may be the means by which you remember your loved one. You will associate a musical theme or lyrics with her. Perhaps you shared a special song; in some way music will help keep the connection to her. There is therapeutic value in music making, but also in music listening. In some way it keeps you connected to the love you have lost. That was the case for one of the widowers I interviewed. He had played the electric guitar for several years prior to the death of his wife. He had been in various bands and singing groups. He commented that he continued to experience a measure of calm when he played his guitar.

"Many individuals use music to deal with bouts of loneliness or to lift their spirits during the day. Even our military uses it to deal with the stress of combat. It is clear that certain forms of music (the type varying for each individual person) affect the brain and our grief work in healthy, positive ways evoke loving memories and bring comfort and respite. There appears to be an increase in brain arousal and mood change when music you like … is played. And it is okay to break sadness with it. It does not have to be a specific kind of music, as in the so-called Mozart effect. Consider playing music the loved one liked to honor him or her and to show love in separation."[16]

There is workout music, traveling music, music to set the mood for romance, music that stirs a patriotic spirit, music through which favorite sports teams are cheered on and the music of worship. Music will help to heal the bereaved mind and mend a broken heart. A couple of the men interviewed for this writing would agree:

I joined a choral society to get out of the house. I also attend concerts. Music brings me into another world. Personally, I like listening to music. It helps me relax. I have become "emotional". I did not used to be that way. Music has opened a door for me that I did not know was there. ZB

I've always enjoyed music. After my wife died I wanted to go to some musicals but I didn't want to go alone. [Not going] really bothered me after a while. RP

I'm not lonely … when I'm engrossed in something, so when I'm in the middle of my music I will not be lonesome. JA

Since my wife died, I have joined three different choral societies. I find singing in a group challenging as I use my mind and voice with others to create beautiful music. My involvement in this activity dissipates my anxiety and gives me a deep sense of satisfaction.

Physical Activity

In a previous chapter I made brief mention of the role that physical activity – hiking, biking, golfing, work out – can play in healing. Let's look at a few real life examples that illustrate the point. Some men I interviewed saw physical activity not as an escape, but as one of the ways they preferred to deal with the grief of their loss. Sometimes this is referred to as movement therapy.

After my wife died, I did have more time. I've always been an active guy so [now] I play more golf. I run [and] go to the gym and workout. SJ

I played tennis; that provided exercise and some associations. RP

I am [now] very intentional about social activities. I joined a hiking club. I've always enjoyed hiking. It was a long tradition for me and my family to go hiking in the fall. I also took kayak lessons and then I took lessons to ride a motorcycle. WZ

I got into golf after my wife passed away. JA

Personally, I started classes in Tai Chi. The slow, disciplined and deliberate movements improve balance and strength. The order of the movements of a routine challenges the memory. The breathing technique of the art also slows the heart rate and reduces blood pressure. I have found that Tai Chi is a very relaxing mental and physical activity. The classes also provide social interaction.

From childhood I've enjoyed riding a bicycle. It's true: once you've learned to ride, you never forget. Over the weeks of riding season, I have been able to build the stamina to ride a distance of thirty miles. The sport is terrifically aerobic and provides longer periods of time to get out of the house to take in God's glorious creation. I admit there is a lot of alone time, but that time can be used to clear the mind and to allow it to operate in default mode if I wish. You might not be thrilled at the start of a ride, but you will be invigorated as a result of the ride.

Recently, I was introduced to pickleball – what some have identified as the fastest growing sport in the U.S. It requires the expenditure of a little more energy than biking. It's a hybrid of tennis, ping-pong and handball, with its own rules and regulations. It's fun, challenging and is usually played in a foursome, offering socialization again. Physical activity can be an effective form of coping. Exercise, for example, is often used as an outlet for anger and aggression. While running is a solitary activity suited for some men, other choose weightlifting or some form of organized sports activity. The playing field, ball diamond, bowling alley or gym may provide opportunities for companionship as well as support.

Counseling

Counseling of the bereaved seems to be on the rise. As one who was a pastor nearly four decades, I do not recall that during that time there was as great an inclination on the part of the bereaved to seek counseling as seems to be the case today. A couple of the questions asked of the interviewees were: "Did you seek individual or group counseling? Why or why not?" The men responded to these questions almost as readily as they had to the question about loneliness. Just a few of their replies reflect their views on what they believe were the benefits or the lack of benefit to them.

I did not feel any need for individual or group counseling. I know what I should say, but I feel as though that I do not need the counseling. In my profession I, have been expected to be self-reliant – an individual who can take care of himself. ZB

I did group therapy almost the whole time. Within the last few months, I've done individual counseling and that has dealt with individual relationships. I learned some things about myself and I realized that I put value and worth in relationships. AM

No, I didn't seek counseling. No! It was offered a couple of times in the particular hospice association – the one that Rhonda used. They offered grief counseling sessions. SJ

I did not seek group or individual counseling because I felt that, again, just by God's grace [and] to think on a spiritual level, you are ready and able to deal with the situation. God gives me his comfort and peace but [even so] that doesn't mean that I didn't grieve her [or] that I didn't miss her dearly. But, I didn't feel like I needed counseling. DM

I did not seek individual counseling not because I was opinionated about it but just because it never happened. I never went to the pastors at the church for counseling. I guess I feel like I never went to the depths of grief that some people do. I never was deeply depressed; crying yes and hurting yes, but I never went emotionally to the point where I felt like I was out of control and I needed somebody to get me thinking straight again. I just concentrated on reading and keeping active ... as much as I could. I didn't know of anyone individually that I would want to go to [in order to talk about my pain]. . . . I went to one group counseling program at the church. I was the only guy and there were eleven women. The man who was running it had never had a death in his family. RP

I coped with Lindsey's loss just by talking to people. I didn't actually sit down and say to anybody, "I need help and counseling please." Maybe I was hoping that I would be able to cut it or handle it – be able to come to grips with and understand what happened. [In the past] I have been able to do that very well ... I didn't seek out counseling except maybe I did do it once I think with a pastor.

I believe [my reluctance to seek counseling is due] perhaps ... part of it is due to stubbornness; [the] desire to just handle things on my own. I think part of that is just that's just the way I am. The other part is that in order to deal with this, I don't drag people through that and I don't believe there's anybody that would be willing to go through that with me. It may very well be that that's the right thing for me to do at this stage. I don't know. I have had both the hospice company who took care of Lindsey at home and the funeral home that took care of her arrangements – they have kept up with me – send me emails; they send me cards in the mail to try to stay in touch and let me know that there are counseling services that are available. So they do a good work in stayed in touch with people even a couple years out and they should, so that people know that they don't have to necessarily go through this alone. JA

No. I didn't feel there was the need to [seek counseling]. Offers were made for help, but I never took anyone up on them. I feel that talking about "things" – any things – not necessarily my loneliness or my wife's passing, not about "the event" but just anything, is therapeutic. I know I have to talk. Talking is the best way to get through all this. LL

I suppose I wanted help in coping with her loss. The grief was certainly [there] and I grieved for weeks after, but that wasn't the most challenging. It was starting to get into rhythm and a new life and a new routine day-to-day. These issues I needed to figure out. WZ

One of the widowers with whom I spoke expressed his opinion about counseling and men:

As far as going to group counseling or grief counseling, I think that it's not the sort of approach men need. Women are used to getting together and talking about everything. They find comfort in just talking things out – not that they try to solve anything – it's just in the fact that they are talking [that they seem to get help]. Men aren't like that. When you get men together in a big group, they're not going to bare their souls to each other. I'm not convinced that men need to talk things out like women. They haven't done it their whole lives, but when it comes to this major loss, people want them to start talking. It just seems to me that counselors are feminizing men when they want to approach men's grief in the same way as they approach grieving women. I know that I'm not going to talk to just anybody about the affairs of my heart. JA

The quotation above seems to align with Lund's findings about the success of counseling received by men: "Many care givers strive to have male mourners respond to loss as do their female counterparts. This is unwise, to say nothing of an almost fruitless goal."[17]

I did not seek counseling. As I stated above, I kept myself busy with various projects and activities that blunted my grief for a while so that I could parse it out in my own time and on my own terms. It's not unusual for large congregations to make group and individual counseling available to the bereaved, so two years after the death of my wife and for sake of gathering information for this book, I did register for a series of eight group counseling sessions that was offered through a church in the area. I wanted to discover what was being said and done to help those who had lost loved ones. The group numbered twenty-three with five men present. Attendance varied over the weeks, but there were always about five times as many women as men. Some of the women had been through the class previously and one man had attended earlier offerings of the course. I discovered that the composition of the group meetings remained about four men to eighteen women throughout the multi-week counseling sessions.

As part of hospice service, many hospice organizations offer grief support *after* the patient dies. Bereavement services vary considerably from agency to agency. Many hospice services offer the kind of counseling and help that one might receive from other social agencies. Some funeral homes include grief counseling and support as part of their services as well.

If you feel that it might be helpful, discuss your grief with a trusted friend, a member of the clergy, a family member or a professional counselor. I would recommend that you not try to tough it out alone. Group or individualized counseling may be beneficial. Although there is tremendous commonality in grief with its attendant aspects and associated feelings, your grief is unique, because you are unique. Find someone whom you will trust and who will listen to you carefully as an individual. Respectfully decline the assistance of anyone who is ready with quick answers to the complicated cares you have. And, by all means, bring this matter to God. God the Holy Spirit is called the Counselor.[18] God will listen and he understands perfectly what you are experiencing. After all, he ordains everything that happens. Use this time in your life to come closer to God.

Routine and Scheduling

If you were not retired at the time of your wife's death, you had a stabilizing force in your life. After a time, you returned to your employment and resumed your routine. For eight to ten hours a day, and perhaps longer, you met your obligations to your employer. If your work included significant travel time, an even greater share of your time was filled with scheduled activity. Some of the men interviewed noted that they returned to work rather quickly considering their loss:

Marla passed away on Tuesday. We had a funeral that following Saturday and I was back in to work the following Monday morning. I think some people just couldn't understand and thought, "How can you be so callous to just be going right back to work?" I needed to be engaged in [my] mind [and to] get back into my normal regular routine as quickly as I could and that really work for me. DM

During her illness I had to keep all the money flowing and ... the bills paid [and] I really enjoy my job. JA

It was good for me to continue to meet my work commitments. I gave my mind to work, so I didn't focus on my sorrow. LL

After Sherri's death, I was back to work within a week. EF

But, if you were retired at the time of your wife's death or have retired since, you have many hours in the day to fill. How will you use those hours? If you have a tendency to withdraw from social interactions, you may be complicating an already difficult situation. Put some structure to your day. If you are still employed, much of that structuring is done for you, but you still have evenings and the weekends. Put some order to them. If you have "nothing" scheduled there's a high probability that you will do "nothing". You could benefit from establishing a routine, which includes both a personal schedule and commitment to others. I suggest that at the close of each day, you have a good idea of what you are going to do on the following day. It's my practice to make a list of activities and obligations each day for the next. My list includes everything from attending classes, reading, sports activities, prayer, choir rehearsal, to medical and dental appointments. That list includes calls I wish to make and bills I have to pay, notes I need to write, household chores, repairs, shopping as well as visit I'd like to make. As I accomplish the assignments I make for myself, I cross through the written line item. At the end of the day I check to see what I have done. The practice gives me a sense of accomplishment. If I can, I'll assign a time for a task. Yes! I do use post-it notes and send myself email notifications and cellphone reminders.

If at all possible, continue to be involved in your church, maintain relationships if you can. Continue or start to volunteer. Being of service to others will serve to heal your heart and mind. "You may find it helpful to set a simple, flexible schedule and try to put some organization into your day. It sometimes helps to put some structure back into your life. Start by setting regular bedtimes, mealtimes, exercise times, and personal time for yourself. This might be difficult at first, but you may find that following a simple and sensible schedule will help you feel more in control of your life and avoid some of the nameless activity and disorientation which often accompanies grief."[19]

Identity

In addition to the loneliness that was discussed earlier, some men also reported having an identity crisis. In so much of their lives they had interactions as a married couple, socializing, decision-making, working and playing together. They had been so close. Their lives were emotionally, physically and socially intertwined. With the death of their wives, their lives were drastically changed in numerous ways. They felt in some respect that their identities had been defined by their wives. Personally, I had a difficult time accepting the reality of my status as a widower. It seemed unreal. I had been married and then single; I had been with someone and then I was alone; I had been part of a couple and then I was not. Certainly, being married did not define me, but to a significant extent my identity was tied to my wife.

Some of the interviewees perhaps overstated their situation. They found themselves wondering who they were and how they fit into the greater scheme of things:

It's a challenge to figure out [my] new identity [since our] identity as a whole was very much tied together. I was aware that changes would come. This is still a work in progress. I am trying to be intentional in [attempting] new things – trying to see what's out there to discover. WZ

It's not typically me; I am no longer the same person I was when I married Lindsey. For [number] years, I as an individual existed [alone]. That was it. [Then I married.] So when you got one of us, you got both of us. We rubbed off on each other . . . I'm not the old Jonathan, because he ceased to exist. I am not him, okay. There's been [number] years of growth in unity and change, so that's one of the things that's very difficult moving forward. It's that you don't know who you are anymore; who you were is gone. That may seem silly but it's true. JA

This is hard and people I know don't realize that you're not the same person. Your wife kind of makes up half of you socially. How they react to you is not the same as the person you were [when] you socialized along with your wife. I never had a lot of guy friends, really. So it's hard for those friends of mine who were friends of ours to know how to react in an awkward situation. I don't feel comfortable interacting with them as much, and they don't know how to interact with me. SJ

What is hard is the absence of physical closeness. I miss being asked about the day, of someone agreeing with me or disagreeing with me. This is hard for so many years I had been married and now it's difficult getting used to the idea of being single. ZB

I'm not used to being single yet. I do and did things on my own, but I'm not experiencing what you would call an identity crisis. EF

Heath observes: "If you have lost your husband or wife, you have, in a sense, lost your world. When we become a couple, we often join every aspect of our lives together – physically, emotionally, and financially. In marriage, spouses' identities become integrally linked together. When one dies, the other usually feels a crippling loss of self. . . In marriage, decisions are often made based on conversation with one's partner. Everything from 'Where shall we live?' to 'What do you want for dinner?' is up for discussion. The 'other' is always *there*, to bounce ideas off of, to argue with, or just to share a laugh over something your child did."[20]

It is true that your identity to some extent had become wrapped up in your wife, and the longer you had been married the more the identities of you and your wife became linked. Having acknowledged that, however, you must realize that your wife, while being a major influence on your identity, was not the sole influence. Your identity has been associated with others since you were born. As your parents' son, you were guided by your parents through the developmental states of infancy and into young adulthood. Along the way your accomplishments in sports or in the classroom or in music all added layers to your identity. Perhaps an outstanding teacher or close friend affected you in ways you can only begin to appreciate. Your profession – plumber, doctor, teacher, mechanic, salesman – identified you further.

Your marriage, of course, introduced a uniquely profound addition to your identity; and when your wife died, while you didn't lose your identity, you were required to redefine the relationship of that one who contributed in such a wonderful way to make you who you are today. She shaped your identity but you will continue to encounter others who will affect your identity. You will have experiences that will affect you in the same way. In some respects, your identity is always changing; in some respects it will not change.

Finally, it is essential that you remember the one way in which your identity is secure; you will always be an image-bearer of God. You are God's creation, stamped with his likeness. What is more, if you are a Christian, you have an identity that never changes. Your experiences may shape you; your values will be redefined, but you will never not be identified with Christ. You may relocate, change employment, grow old or become ill; you may prosper materially or become poor, but your identity as an image-bearer of God and your status as a new creation in Christ will not change. These realities should be your source of stability and identity. You will eventually lose all the time bound persons and experiences that so often bear on your identity but you will not lose the most important identity of all.

Chapter Seventeen

What You Should Know

Where there is no guidance people fall, but in an abundance of counselors there is safety. (Proverbs 11:14)

Some of the suggestions in this chapter – like those in previous chapters – will relate to those of you who have already become widowers. If you, on the other hand, are anticipating your wife's death, you may still have time to implement some of these suggestions if you have not yet done so. Part of getting on with living after your wife has died is to attend to legal and financial matters. You had to arrange for your wife's interment, which required financial and legal considerations. You had to pay for the funeral itself or to make arrangements for payment. You will need to deal with other financial and legal issues in the days and months ahead. Today it is difficult to deal with a matter that is exclusively legal without there being potential financial ramifications. The reverse is true also; the financial decisions you make may have legal consequences. It is a good idea to give some thought now about how you will discharge the responsibilities related to your wife's death. I have mentioned both the legal and financial concerns you will face but there are other personal and practical matters you will need to address as well. This concluding chapter will be ordered to consider the legal issues first, followed by the financial and then the personal and practical.

Legal Considerations

I thought that it would be helpful in this section to approach the material by asking a few questions about legal matters, and then to offer simple answers. I am not an attorney and would not presume to offer legal advice. Nothing that I say in this chapter should be taken as legal advice. My purpose at this point is to open an awareness of issues that widowers and those expecting in the near future to be widowers will certainly face.

We enjoy many benefits from living in a land governed by law, but such benefits come with legal obligations. It is nearly impossible in today's world to navigate the legal waters alone. There seems no end to the making, interpreting and applying of the laws;

you and I cannot begin to know and much less to understand them all. The legal profession has its specialties as does any other profession. The law is complicated and if you are not an attorney practicing in the area of estate and probate (and even if you are) it is wise and well for you to seek the services of a competent attorney. If you do not currently have an attorney, you should take steps to engage one as soon as possible. As in any profession, so in the legal profession; professional skills, knowledge and abilities vary. Ask a friend or family member for recommendations. Talk to several people; get their thoughts about what kind of legal expertise you may require.

Death Certificates

After the death of your wife, you will need to obtain death certificates. What is a death certificate? It is a legal document. It is issued by a county coroner's office to the family of the deceased. A death certificate provides the deceased person's information and specifies the date, time and the cause of the death. It also states the disposition of the body, whether buried or cremated. The purpose of a death certificate is to provide proof of death in dealing with financial and governmental organizations. It makes the transfer of inheritance possible and "authorizes the family to collect insurance and other benefits."[1] You may need several death certificates. Initially, your funeralist should offer some of these to you as part of your funeral costs and should ask about the number of death certificates you think you might need. If you need additional certificates, you may get them at the city hall or a bureau of vital statistics of the county where the death took place. There is a nominal charge for each additional certificate. You will need the death certificates to show proof of death in order to redeem insurance policies, to close or change the name on jointly held savings accounts, to transfer jointly held property, to "roll over" your wife's Roths, IRAs, etc. into your accounts of which you were the beneficiary. If you and your wife owned property together, a death certificate and possibly other documentation will be required to place property into your name. You may need one to apply for your wife's Social Security Death Benefits. A token dollar amount is available from Social Security for burial expenses, but you have to request that benefit. When you are transferring ownership of your wife's assets, you may be required at some juncture to provide a signature guarantee. There is a level of verification beyond notarizing. A signature guarantee is used for the transfer of some securities, stocks and investment vehicles. Most banks and brokerage agencies provide for these signatures.

A Will

What is a will? It is a legal document in which the writer of the will, the testator, expresses his or her wishes about the distribution of assets and the care of minor children. It identifies an executor who is responsible to see that the provisions of the will are carried out. The executor should pay outstanding financial obligations of the deceased from the assets of the estate. If you do not have a will, you should look into having one made as soon as possible. Fifty-six percent of the population dies "intestate", that is, without a will.[2] If your wife has no will, her estate will be disposed according the laws of the state in which you live. The distribution of your wife's assets is done by the probate court.

Probate Court

What is probate? What if your wife did not have a will? How will her estate be settled? Probate is a legal process of settling the estate of someone who has died. The purpose of the probate court is legally "to administer the estate, to pay outstanding obligations, and to distribute remaining assets to the proper recipients."[3] The probate court will appoint a person (individual or a corporate entity) to serve as the executor or administrator to settle the estate of the deceased. If you as the (former) husband wish to be appointed the executor of your late wife's estate, you must apply to the court. The executor or administrator becomes responsible to transfer assets. Transfer of assets may not be what the deceased might have desired, however. The probate court "provides an orderly process for the presentment of claims against the estate, and also sets a fixed time period to assert claims."[4] If your wife had her separate checking account that had no joint ownership or beneficiary for example, and she died intestate, you would have to go through probate to have the money in that checking account transferred into your own banking account.

Assets, however, do not have to be transferred through the use of the probate courts exclusively; probate is just one of a number of ways to achieve transfer of assets. Probate may be avoided through the use of a living revocable trust, which is a trust created during the lifetime of the grantor/settlor and into which assets are placed during a lifetime. Probate may be avoided also if beneficiaries are named in investment instruments. "A reversible living trust may also be named as the beneficiary on a beneficiary designation provided by the applicable financial institutions."[5] Some securities, stocks, money funds, etc. have TOD (Transfer on Death) or Pay On Death (POD) provisions which automatically distribute the assets of the deceased according to his or her prescribed assignments. Sometimes TODs specify dollar amounts; sometimes they specify a percentage of the assets to be transferred. You can also make direct lifetime gifts to your beneficiaries. Assets that are transferred through probate face delays; the process can be rather costly, and all the actions taken by the probate court are a matter of public record. If dollars, time and privacy are of concern to you, you will try to avoid probate. Revocable living trusts, lifetime gifts and TOD transfers are private, in most cases without cost and much quicker than probate. You should try to minimize your administrative costs in the transfer of your wife's assets. Again, if your wife had a will, after her death, you or someone on your behalf should file your wife's will with the clerk of the probate court. If you are the executor of your wife's will, you must see to it that her will is executed as she specified. Perhaps she bequeathed monies, furnishings, clothing or jewelry, etc. to persons named in her will. These are all matters to which you will need to attend.

Transference of investments into your retirement accounts may be only as complicated as the number of funds or accounts that your wife had, or you and your wife had together. It may be that if a number of accounts are managed by one financial institution that you will need only one death certificate for that managing agency. You may discover, however, that some financial services require a separate death certificate for each specific account number. It took me about two years to conclude these matters with various brokerage companies.

Power of Attorney

What is a power of attorney (POA)? A power of attorney is a written document in which a person grants someone else, the legal right to represent or to act on his or her behalf. It authorizes the one who has the POA to conduct legal and financial business. There are basically two types of power of attorney: a legal and financial power of attorney; and a health care power of attorney (See below for the provisions of the health care power of attorney.).

What is the purpose of a legal and financial power of attorney? A legal and financial power of attorney is an official document that grants someone the right to make legal and financial decisions of behalf of the one who granted that power of attorney. In the event of a disability or some other incapacity for example, the one who has legal power of attorney (the agent) for another may exercise the right to pay bills and otherwise manage the assets of the one who granted him or her that power. If there is no legal power of attorney named, the assets of an incapacitated person cannot be managed until the probate court appoints a guardian of the estate. As I mentioned above, probate may be a time consuming and costly process. An appointed guardian is required to act in the best interests of the ward of the court, but must obtain court approval to expend funds on behalf of the estate and must make periodic reports to the court. It is far and away preferable for you to grant legal and financial power of attorney to someone you know and trust, who would take actions that would align with the your wishes. You as husband to your wife do not have the power of attorney for her automatically. Such power must be granted in a document to you by your wife, signed and notarized designating you as her agent. Does the law require that a will be filed with the probate court upon the death of the testator? Yes it does, but if *all* of your wife's assets are jointly owned or have beneficiaries, there may not be need for probate administration.[6]

JTWROS

What is JTWROS and what are the advantages in holding property with a JTWROS provision? JTWROS means simply, "Joint Tenants With Right Of Survivorship". If you and your wife own a house or car or other kinds of property, and if either one of you dies, the property transfers immediately to the surviving spouse. This is another way ownership of property may be transferred privately, quickly, and with no or little costs. For example, if you and your wife own a car and the title line showed included the letters JTWROS, when either of you dies, the car becomes the property of the other. If, on the other hand, those letters were not present and either of you were to die, the car would become part of the estate of the one who died. If you survived your wife, you would not be able to get clear title of the car until your wife's estate would be settled. If you and your wife wished that the car become the property of the surviving spouse, then JTWROS would be the method to use. Personally, it became a complicated matter for me to transfer my car into my own name since my wife's name was also on the title without the JTWROS provision. The car had become part of her estate. I needed her death certificate and other documentation to acquire a new car title when I moved into another state.

Taxes

What about taxes? How does my wife's death affect my tax obligations? Now that you are a widower, you will experience a year of "firsts". If you filed federal, state, and local income taxes jointly, you will still need to file jointly in the year of your wife's death. If you both became residents of another state during your wife's last year, you may have to pay proportionate taxes in the states where you lived. What if you had filed your taxes separately? Does the deceased have tax obligations? The answer is "Yes". Your wife in that case would still owe taxes and a final 1040 would have to be filed on her behalf. Payment could come from her estate.

Health Care Power of Attorney

What is health care power of attorney? How is it different than a legal power of attorney? A health care power of attorney is an official document that grants someone (the agent) the authority to make health care decisions on behalf of the one (the principal) who granted that power. Those decisions may be made when the person who granted that power is no longer able (physically or mentally) to make health care decisions for him or herself. Moreover, a health care power of attorney gives the right to someone to speak for another when that person can no longer speak for herself. Additionally, the person who has healthcare power of attorney may gather private and protected health care information on behalf of the grantor immediately or at any other time. You and your wife may have had a conversation about measures not to be taken in case of her physical and or mental declension and death. You may have discussed what kind of treatment should be received or declined in the event that she could no longer speak for herself. Perhaps you had health care power of attorney to make decisions for her which under normal circumstances she would have made for herself. "A healthcare power of attorney is needed to ensure that you, the husband, have the authority to make critical healthcare decisions for your wife."[7] If you have a healthcare POA, you have the decision-making authority, you have the power to make all medical care decisions up to and including end of life decisions. A healthcare POA is not the same as a legal and financial POA, but both kinds of POA terminate upon the death of the grantor. When my own mother was no longer able to make legal, financial and medical decisions for herself, I had legal power of attorney, but my sister, who was in the medical profession, had health care power of attorney for her.

Will I Have To Have A New Will?

Most likely you will not need to make a new will. "Legal documents do not change because of a death."[8] A will should be goal-driven. Ask yourself: "What do I want to achieve by having a will?" You certainly want to transfer your assets and in some cases make sure that specific items pass on to those whom you wish. You may also want to bequeath gifts to various charities or agencies. Your wishes should be spelled out in your will. If your wife was the executor of your estate, you may wish to update your will, but in most cases, an alternate executor is named in your will in the event of the inability of the primary executor becoming unable to fulfill duties. The same is true with respect to beneficiaries. Wills routinely name contingency beneficiaries in the event that those named as primary beneficiaries no longer live. A device called *per stirpes* provides that the children of heirs receive an equal portion of what their parents would have received. "The death of a loved one does not necessitate making a new will; it is a time to review rather than to redo [a will]."[9] Rasnick's advice is to write a will as if you were going to die tomorrow.[10] You must determine if anything needs to be changed. If, upon reviewing your will you realize that it no longer reflects your wishes, it is time to make changes.

When Must Decisions Be Made

We might put the question another way: "Is there a certain window of time within which particular legal action must be taken after the death of a spouse?" The answer to that question is, "Not so much anymore." It used to be that estate taxes had to be filed within nine months of a person's death. This is no longer the case in the state where I currently live, but it may be the case where you live. You will have to discover what the requirements are in your own location. Federal estate taxes are still due within nine months of a person's death. Check with a tax attorney; non-spouse heirs of traditional IRAs and Roths must comply with required withdrawal schedules.

Financial Concerns

Sometimes a man does not manage the financial side of the house during his marriage; he has left those matters to his wife. Suddenly, when he has lost his wife, he is faced with a new administrative task. Perhaps you did take care of the money matters in your marriage. Good! That is to your advantage now, but even if you did take care of the money matters in your marriage, you may not have the emotional energy to tackle the added financial responsibilities that are specific to the death of a spouse. Having said that, you should attend to the financial side of things as soon as you can, even if it requires getting the assistance of an attorney or financial advisor.

If your wife's departure was anticipated, you may have had opportunity to talk with her about various accounts, charges, bills and other financial obligations that she had handled. If you are not yet a widower and are able to have a conversation with your wife about financial matters, by all means do so. It is time to talk about powers of attorney. You have the opportunity to make changes to the titles of property, to add co-owners, to add or change beneficiaries. As you read these suggestions you may think that they are cold and unfeeling. Discussions like this will be very difficult, but you must have them for the benefit of all who are left behind. It will help you immeasurably to have names of all the financial institutions and their agents you use; to have account numbers and statements generated from those accounts; copies of insurances policies, and other important legal and financial documents. After your wife's death, you will need to cancel the credit cards that your wife had. Charge accounts left unused will still incur interests on the unpaid balances and generate fees and those fees and interest charges can mount up quickly. Most major credit card companies provide customer service numbers for help in managing accounts. If your wife has managed any accounts online, be sure to have a copy of her user names and passwords. If she had her own checking account, it would be well to keep it open for six months for refunds or for checks to clear.

We live at a time when much business and record keeping is done electronically. Your wife may have scheduled monthly services or shipments of products which she will no longer need. If she used autofill for her prescriptions, you will need to cancel those prescriptions and end the autofill service. Along that same line, you may wish to cancel magazine subscriptions, which renew automatically. You will need to attend to anything that takes place on a pre-scheduled arrangement. Beautician appointments, doctor and dentist appointments fall into this category. If your wife had her own car, she had insurance. You would want to cancel her policy; and if she was insured when driving your car, it would be well to remove her name as one of the insured. Doing so could affect your insurance premiums. You may want to notify the members of clubs, associations, organizations and societies to which your wife belonged. If your wife's death was sudden and/or unexpected, there may be those with whom your wife associated who do not know of her death. There are probably scores of little things that will surface over the weeks after her passing that should be addressed. Has your wife left anything at the cleaners? Are there library books that should be returned? Did she use a cell phone? You will need to cancel the service unless you want a second cell phone. Did she have supplemental health care coverage or an employee death benefit? Did she have life insurance which included an immediate cash voucher in the event of her death? Is your wife entitled to death benefits for her military service? I admit that the mention of these matters barely scratches the surface of what you may have to take care of on the business and financial side.

Personal Concerns

In chapters eleven, fifteen and sixteen I broached the subjects of the social, emotional and physical issues that you will face as a newly-widowed man. At some time you will resume much of your earlier life routine. Some pieces of it may be in place sooner than others. Again, your process, your journey is unique; you are on your own timetable. Some of the questions you faced because of the death of your wife, you now need to make sure are answered on your own behalf. Is there information that others would need to know in the event of *your* death? These concerns may take on added significance because you are now alone. Do you have information that you alone possess which would be needed by someone else in settling your estate? In your wife's absence, who will fulfill what your wife may have managed if you are unable to make these decisions for yourself? Who will fill that role for you now? Do you have a living will? Have you designated anyone to make decisions on your behalf when you are no longer able to make them for yourself? Have you authorized someone to speak for you if you were to become unable to speak for yourself? Perhaps you had an understanding with your wife about these matters. Have you had a conversation with the person(s) who may have to speak or act on your behalf? You and I do not know the specifics of our personal futures, but we need to prepare for what is certainly inevitable. My counsel would be to make these choices and have these conversations while you are able.

End of life issues often divide families. You need to communicate and manage the information you desire your family to know. They need to understand your wishes so that there is not confusion or conflict after you have left this life. You should be intentional, specific and prompt in communicating your desires to your family. You will be helping your heirs tremendously if you provide them the same kind of information about your legal and financial matters as you gathered from your wife. Too many men in your situation have praiseworthy intentions but postpone taking the actions that are required. Don't be one of them. It would be advantageous to your heirs to write a legacy letter in which you spell out your wishes concerning legal, financial and personal matters. Let someone know where to access your passwords to accounts, locations of important documents, and the account numbers of various investments, savings and insurance policies you may have. Do you have a safety deposit box? Where is it located; where are the keys? Where are the titles to your vehicles; where are the deeds to your real estate? How can someone locate your birth and marriage certificates? Have you let someone know how to manage your utilities accounts or at least how to access those account numbers? Do you have a cemetery plot? Is it paid for? Where is it located? What are your wishes regarding the disposition of your body and what you want included when you are funeralized? Do you have a funeral policy and if so, with whom? Where is it located? Be intentional in these matters. When is a better time than right now to get started? Take the next steps; go ahead and do it!

Do you have a charity or a religious affiliation that could benefit from your support? You have the opportunity to advance the mission of the organizations and institutions that are dear to your heart. Perhaps you have thought about making a monetary contribution. In Christian circles, the question is sometimes asked, "How much of my income should I give to the church?" Whereas the standard replied to that question is ten percent, the giving of the average Christian is around 2.4%. Less than 1% of giving to the church or parachurch organizations comes through bequeathal or legacies.[11] It is relatively rare that people give gifts to religious organizations. This is shocking! You may have the opportunity to make a significant contribution to the congregation or denomination of your choice, and designate funds for special uses. You cannot take your monies with you, but you could entrust some of it to those who will apply them to worthy causes. In all of your planning about the disposition and disbursal of your estate, don't forget your religious and charitable institutions.

Advance Directives

Have you put Advance Directives into place? Most states recognize what has come to be called, "Advance Directives". There are two kinds of advance directives: (1) a living will declaration, and (2) a health care power of attorney. A living will is a legal document, which issues a directive to a physician or medical care provider regarding comfort, care and your wishes not to pursue treatment in the event of terminal illness or permanent coma. It comes into effect when one is no longer able to make medical decisions for him or herself. A living will does not replace a will which is used to appoint an executor to manage a person's estate after death.

A health care power of attorney on the other hand, grants decision-making power to someone to make all medical care decisions up to and including end of life decisions. It is well for you to have both a living will and to grant someone a health care power of attorney for yourself.

Thoughts To Conclude

You chose to read a book entitled *A Widower's Way* and I thank you for reading it to this point. It is my prayer and hope that in some small way my comments have served to move you along your way. You have been and will continue to be on a journey. You were joined in your journey by your wife and you now must continue it without her. As in any journey, there are detours and delays. People on a journey may become impatient because of those delays, but waiting is part of the experience. At times you feel as though you are making wonderful progress and at other times you may feel that you have come to a complete standstill. The same must be said of an emotional journey. There will be those moments when you doubt that you have made any progress at all in adjusting to the loss of your wife. You can never get beyond your thoughts of her or move on as though the years of your walking together did not happen. You made your way together, encouraged, supported and shaped each other. You have been changed by her presence and you will be changed by her absence. You were a source of strength for her and she was the same for you. You will miss her for the variety of ways in which she shaped **you**, but you will move forward. It is therapeutic to look at where you have been and it is wise to look at the road ahead. In the days following her death you will do plenty of looking back; you need also to look forward. Remember! This is a journey. It is A Widower's Way. You *will* make definite progress. It will be imperceptible at times but you will make your way. Others will come alongside to help you, to encourage you and support you. At times your way will be winding and uphill and you will wonder if you can make it. Yes! By the grace of God you will make it. Yours is a unique journey. Your journey is as unique as you are. Recognize your uniqueness, go at your own pace and resist the pull to make comparisons with others. It is your journey, your way. Finally, you do not have to walk alone. You may call to God for his help. He will walk with you. God will not refuse your sincere request for wisdom, comfort and peace. He will grant these to you and many more amazing benefits when you place your life in his hands.

ENDNOTES

[1] Family.jrank.org/pages/1753/widowhood-demography-widowed.html.
[2] *ibid.*

Chapter One: How This Started

[1] CHOP is an acronym for cyclophosphamide, hydroxydaunorubicin, oncovin and prednisone, a standard combination of drugs used as a chemotherapy regimen to combat non-Hodgkin lymphoma and other cancers.

[2] It is well, if at all possible, for you to accompany your wife as she goes for her doctors' appointments and treatments. Your presence alone tells her that you care and are with her during her experience. You will be able to take notes and recall directions or explanations given to her which she may not readily recall.

Chapter Two: A New Normal

[1] John 9:2
[2] John 9:3
[3] 2 Corinthians 12:8-9
[4] Genesis 1:26, 31
[5] The Westminster Shorter Catechism in Modern English, questions and answers 10 and 13.
[6] Romans 5:12
[7] The Westminster Shorter Catechism in Modern English 19.
[8] Genesis 2:16-17; 3:1-7, 16-19
[9] Letters of John Calvin, 4:331.
[10] Ryle, J.C., Sickness, Matthias Media, Kingsford, Australia, 2005, p. 10.
[11] Romans 8:28
[12] Psalm 119:71
[13] Psalm 119:67
[14] 2 Kings 15:5; 2 Chronicles 26:16-21
[15] 2 Corinthians 1:3-5
[16] Colossians 3:10
[17] Hebrews 4:15-16
[18] Romans 15:4

[19] Boice, James M., Come To The Waters: Daily Bible Devotions For Spiritual Refreshment, P&R Publishing, P.O. Box 817, Phillipsburg, New Jersey, 2017, p.74, March 6.

[20] *ibid.*, p. 75, March 7.

[21] Acts 17:26-27

Chapter Three: Wife's Decline

[1] Wolfelt, Alan D., Finding Words, Compassion Press: The Center for Loss and Life Transition, Fort Collins, CO, p. 112.

[2] Psalm 23:4

[3] Romans 8:28

[4] Leviticus 21:10-11

[5] Ezekiel 24:15-24

Chapter Four: Time Together

[1] Genesis 50:24-26

[2] Exodus 13:19; Joshua 24:32

[3] 1 Kings 21:19

[4] 2 Samuel 12:9

[5] The way the word "kill" is written in the Hebrew language suggests that David caused Uriah to be killed.

[6] Exodus 21:13; Numbers 35:22-25; Deuteronomy 19:1-10; Joshua 20:1-9

[7] Genesis 9:6

[8] Martin, Al, Grieving, Hope and Solace: When a loved one dies in Christ. Cruciform Press, 2011, p. 103-104.

Chapter Five: Hospice

[1] Beresford, Larry, The Hospice Handbook: A Complete Guide, Little, Brown and Company, NY, 1993, p. 3.

[2] *ibid.*, p. xvii.

[3] *ibid.*, p. xxiv; p. 8.

[4] *ibid.*, p. 5.

[5] *ibid.*

[6] *ibid.*, p. 9.

[7] *ibid.*, p. 15.

[8] *ibid.,* p. 17.
[9] *ibid.,* p. 18.
[10] *ibid.* italics mine
[11] *ibid.,* pp. 19-20.
[12] *ibid.,* p. 20.
[13] *ibid.,* p. 22.

Chapter Six: The Reality of Death

[1] Psalm 104:29
[2] Job 3:14-15
[3] Psalm 146:4
[4] Matthew 22:23; Acts 23:8
[5] Deuteronomy 25:5-7
[6] Matthew 22:30
[7] Romans 7:2
[8] Matthew 22:30
[9] Genesis 2:18-25
[10] Matthew 19:3-9; Mark 10:5-10
[11] Matthew 19:4-5
[12] Ephesians 5:29
[13] 1 Peter 3:7
[14] Genesis 1:28
[15] Genesis 9:1, 7
[16] Malachi 2:15
[17] 1 Corinthians 7:5
[18] Hebrews 13:4
[19] 1 Corinthians 7:14
[20] Ephesians 6:10-18

Chapter Seven: Meeting with the Funeralist

[1] Federal Trade Commission, https://smartasset.com/life-insurance/how-much-does-the-average-funeral-cost.

Chapter Eight: Visitation and Funeral

[1] Genesis 23:1-4

2 *ibid.*

3 Genesis 25:7-10

4 Genesis 3:28-29; 49:31

5 Genesis 49:31

6 Genesis 46:4

7 Exodus 13:19; Joshua 24:32

8 Joshua 24:30

9 1 Samuel 25:1

10 1 Kings 2:34.

11 2 Kings 21:18

12 2 Kings 23:30

13 2 Chronicles 16:14

14 Jackson, Edgar N., The Christian Funeral: Its Meaning: Its Purpose and Its Modern Practice, Channel Press, NY, p. 4.

15 Acts 9:37

16 John 11:44; 20:5-8

17 John 12:3-5

18 Acts 9:37; Matthew 9:18, 23-24, cf. 2 Chronicles 16:14

19 Luke 7:11-15

20 Leviticus 10:1-4, Acts 5:1-11; Edgar, George B., The International Standard Bible Encyclopedia, Wm. B. Eerdmans Publishing Company, Grand Rapids, MI, copyright 1939, p. 529.

21 *Ibid.*

22 Moody, Raymond and Arcangel, Dianne, Life After Loss: Conquering Grief and finding Hope, HarperCollins Publishers, Inc. NY, 2001, p. 37.

23 Jackson, p. 23

24 Ecclesiastes 3:2

25 Ecclesiastes 7:2

26 James 4:13-15

27 Genesis 2:17

28 Genesis 3:19

29 Romans 5:12

30 Romans 3:23

31 Romans 6:23

32 Hebrews 9:27

[33] Ephesians 2:1

[34] John 3:36

[35] Romans 7:24

[36] Jackson, p. 7

[37] *Ibid.*, p. 15, quoting Robert Fulton in the book Death and Identity, Wiley, 1965.

[38] *Ibid.*

[39] *Ibid.*, p. 17

[40] *Ibid.*, p. 24, quoting Eric Lindemann.

[41] Westminster Shorter Catechism in Modern English; Psalm 86:9; Isaiah 60:21; Romans 11:36; 1 Corinthians 6:20; 10:31

[42] 1 Corinthians 10:31

[43] Deuteronomy 32:39; 1 Samuel 2:6; 2 Kings 5:7; Psalms 90:3

[44] Psalm 90:10

[45] James 4:14

[46] 2 Corinthians 5:10; Hebrews 9:27

[47] John 11:25

[48] John 5:26-29

[49] John 6:40

[50] Romans 6:5

[51] Jackson Edgar N., The Christian Funeral: Its Meaning, Its Purpose and Its Modern Practice, p. 29.

[52] *ibid.*, p. 30-31.

[53] Oates, Wayne, E., Grief, Transition and Loss: A Pastor's Practical Guide, Augsburg, Fortress, Minneapolis, MN, p. 27.

[54] Ecclesiastes 3:4

[55] Ecclesiastes 7:2-4

[56] 1 Thessalonians 4:13

[57] Ecclesiastes 3:4

[58] Revelation 21:4

Chapter Nine: What is Next?

[1] Jensen, Amy H., Healing Grief, 1995; Karnes, B., My Friend, I Care, BK Books, Vancouver, WA, 2009, p. 12.

Chapter Ten: Unanticipated Death

[1] Peter Saul on Youtube.com.

[2] Wolfelt, Alan D., Finding Words, Compassion Press: The Center for Loss and Life Transition, Fort Collins, CO, p. 112.

[3] Oates, Wayne, E., Grief, Transition and Loss: A Pastor's Practical Guide, Augsburg Fortress, Minneapolis, MN, p. 20.

[4] Dr Kriss Wiant, Ph.D., psychologist, interview on March 21, 2018.

[5] *Oates.*, p. 21.

[6] Westminster Shorter Catechism in Modern English 19.

[7] Leviticus 11:1-47

[8] Mark 7:21-23.98

[9] Genesis 4:1-16

[10] fbi.gov/newspressrel/press-releases/fbi-releases/2017-crime-statistics

[11] google.com/search?q=how+many+acts+of+violence (post date 092119)

[12] Genesis 9:6

[13] Romans 13:1-5

[14] Romans 12:19 quoted from Deuteronomy 32:35 LXX.

[15] 2 Corinthians 5:10.

[16] Hebrews 9:27

[17] http://www.questia.com/newspaper/1P2-39553954/u-s-suiciide-rate-soars-to-a-30-year-high.

[18] 1 Samuel 31:4-6

[19] 1 Kings 16:18

[20] 2 Samuel 17:23

[21] Matthew 26:47-51

[22] Matthew 27:3-5

[23] James 1:20

[24] Health, Judy, No Time For Tears: Coping with Grief in a Busy World, second edition, Chicago Review Press, Inc., Chicago, IL, 2015, pp. 211-212.

[25] 1 Peter 3:18

Chapter Eleven: What is New

[1] Lund 148: Casertam M.S. and Lund, D.A., Intrapersonal Resources and the Effectiveness of Self-Help Groups for Bereaved Older Adults., *The Gerontologist*, 33, 1993, pp. 619-629.

[2] http://www.nytimes.com/2006/06/01fashion/thursdaystyles/01marry.html. (search results position=5)

[3] Corinthians 7:39

[4] Romans 7:1-3

[5] Heath, Judy, No Time For Tears: Coping with Grief in a Busy World, second edition, Chicago Review Press, Inc., Chicago, IL, 2015, p. 193.

[6] O'Hara, Kathleen, A Grief Like No Other: Surviving the Violent death of Someone You Love, Marlow and Company, NY, 2006, pp. 186-187.

Chapter Twelve How Do You Think About Grief?

[1] 1 Samuel 30:1-5

[2] 2 Samuel 1:12, 17-27

[3] 2 Samuel 3:31-35

[4] 2 Samuel 4:8-12

[5] 2 Samuel13:30-32

[6] 2 Samuel 12:20-23

[7] 2 Samuel 18:33

[8] http://griefandmourning.com/grief-and-mourning-distinguished.

[9] Gaffin, Jean, Y., "Weeping Tarries for the Night," in New Horizon's Magazine, June 2018.

[10] Jackson, Edgar N., The Christian Funeral: Its Meaning, Its Purpose and Its Modern Practice, Channel Press, NY, p. 35.

[11] Heath, p. 142.

[12] *ibid.*, p. 91.

[13] Lund 148: Casertam M.S. and Lund, D.A., Intrapersonal Resources and the Effectiveness of Self-Help Groups for Bereaved Older Adults., *The Gerontologist*, 33, 1993, p. 37.

[14] Doka, Kenneth, Grieving Beyond Gender: Understanding the Ways Men and Women Grieve. Routledge Publishing, Oxfordshire, UK 2010 p. 133.

[15] Janssen, J. Scott, Understanding the Way Men Grieve. Social work today.com /archive/exc_8016.shtml.

[16] Heath, p. 141.

[17] Neeld, Elizabeth H., LegacyConnect.com/inspire/do-men-grieve-differently-from.

[18] Konigsberg, Ruth, Davis, The Truth About Grief: the Myth of Its Five steps and the New Science of Loss, Simon and Shuster, New York, p. 94. Konigsberg summarizes the developments of Kübler-Ross' thinking on death and dying and traces the origin – though debated – of the five stages of dying.

[19] *ibid.*, p. 96.

[20] *ibid.*, p. 87.

[21] Kelley, Patricia, Companion to Grief: Finding Consolation When Someone You Love Has Died, Simon and Schuster, NY, 1997, p. 37.

[22] ibid.

[23] Dr. Kriss Wiant, Ph. D. psychologist, interview on March 21, 2018

[24] Konigsberg, p. 45.

[25] Kelley, p. 29.

[26] *ibid.*

[27] *ibid.*, p. 31.

[28] Prigerson, Holly G. and Maciejewski, Paul K., "Grief and Acceptance as Opposite Sides of the Same Coin: Setting a Research Agenda to Study Peaceful Acceptance of Loss," in the *British Journal of Psychiatry* 193 (December 2008): 453-57.

[29] Isaiah 53:3

[30] Isaiah 53:4

[31] Isaiah 53:8

[32] Isaiah 53:10

[33] John 11:35

[34] John 11:33

[35] Matthew 27:37-39

[36] Hebrews 4:25

[37] Revelation 21:4

[38] 1 Thessalonians 4:13

[39] Heath, p. 164 where Heath lists nearly twenty indicators of grief reconciliation.

[40] http://www.connect.legacy.com/inspire/the-work-of- +Rando%2C+Therese.

[41] Zonnebelt-Smeenge, Susan J., and DeVries, Robert C., Getting to the Other Side of Grief: Overcoming the Loss of a Spouse. Baker Books, Grand Rapids, MI, 1998, p. 65.

[42] *ibid.*

[43] "Absence of Grief," The Psychoanalytical Quarterly 6 (1937): 12-22.

[44] Events organized throughout the country by those who have been widowed to express their grief collectively and publically. Mourners travel to these events to support one another and to receive support in their grieving.

[45] Konigsberg, p. 68.

Chapter Thirteen: The Emotional Side

[1] Reiss, Michele A., Lessons in Loss and Living: Hope and Guidance for Confronting Serious Illness and Grief, Hyperion, New York, NY 2010 p. 163.

[2] ibid., p. 192.

[3] Grieving with Hope Seminar material, Parkside Church, Chagrin Falls, OH, Spring 2017.

[4] Oates, Wayne, E., Grief, Transition and Loss: A Pastor's Practical Guide, Augsburg Fortress, Minneapolis, MN p.17.

[5] Health discusses this matter on page 199 of her cited book.

[6] Lund, Dale, A. (ed.), Men Coping with Grief, Baywood Publishing Company, Inc., Amityville, NY, 2001, p. 148.

[7] angusreid.org/social-isolation-canada, a study on loneliness and isolation in Canada.

[8] http://www.parentingpatch.com/loneliness-increase-risk-premature-death-among-seniors

[9] Kelley, Patricia, Companion to Grief: Finding Consolation When Someone You Love Has Died, Simon and Schuster, NY, 1997, p. 31.

[10] Sood, Amit. The Mayo Clinic Guide To Stress-Free Living, DaCapo Press, Boston MA, 2013, p. 6.

[11] ibid., p. 7.

Chapter Fourteen: The Physical Side

[1] Reiss, p. 163.

[2] Heath, p. 10-11.

[3] https://www.sleepless.org/grief and sleep/how-does-grief-affect-sleep.

[4] Heath, p. 8.

[5] Kelley, p. 119.

[6] Oates, Wayne, E., Grief, Transition and Loss: A Pastor's Practical Guide, Augsburg Fortress, Minneapolis, MN p. p.23 quoting Clifford Kuhn, M.D.

[7] https://www.thecut.com/2015/11/science-of-longterm-couples-who-die-together.

[8] https://www.books.google.comm/books?id=F7S40AAAQBAJ&pq=PT28&1pg=PT 28&dq= will+experience+a=Serious.

[9] https://www.eurekalert.org/pub_releases/2018-11/ru-glt110918.php.

[10] Psalm 139:2-3

[11] Matthew 6:27

[12] http://www.widowshope.org/first-steps/these-are-the-statistics/{item 14}.

[13] See Heath for her list of possible physical responses to grief, pp. 10-11.

[14] Heath, p. 140.

[15] Oates, p. 21.

Chapter Fifteen: Recovery and Closure

[1] Malachi 3:6

[2] Moody, Raymond, Jr., and Arcangel, Dianne, Life After Loss: Conquering Grief and Finding Hope, HarperCollins Publishers, Inc. 2001, p. 86.

[3] Jenkins, Bill, S., What To Do When The Police Leave. WBJ Press, Richmond, VA p. 66.

[4] Prend, Ashley David, ACSW, The Myth of Closure in Journeys Newsletter, February, 1999, produced by the Hospice Foundation of America.

[5] O'Hara, p. 120.

[6] Gaffin, Jean, Y., "Weeping Tarries for the Night," in New Horizon's Magazine, June 2018.

Chapter Sixteen: What You Can Do

[1] Lagrand, Louis E., Healing Grief, finding Peace: 101 Ways to Cope with the death of Your Loved One, Sourcebooks, Inc. Naperville, IL 2011, pp. 269-270.

[2] Doka, K., *The Therapeutic Bookshelf*, Omega, 21, pp. 321-326.

[3] Lund, Dale, A. (ed.), Men Coping with Grief, Baywood Publishing Company, Inc., Amityville, NY, 2001, p. 45.

[4] *ibid.*, p. 43.

[5] Wiant.

[6] LaGrand, p. 105.

[7] Jenkins, Bill, S., What To Do When The Police Leave. WBJ Press, Richmond, VA 2001, p. 66.

[8] Taylor, Dale, B., Biomedical Foundations of Music as Therapy, 2nd ed., Barton Publications, Eau Claire WI 2010, p. 103.

[9] Ellen Antes, certified neurological music therapist, interview on November 27, 2017.

[10] Taylor, p. 99.

[11] When singer Randy Travis had a stroke, music therapists were enlisted to help him regain the ability to sing. When Congresswoman Gabby Gifford of Arizona was shot and lost ability to speak, music therapy was used to help her regain that ability.

[12] Taylor, p. 174. What goes on in the brain when someone hears music? For one thing, "Epinephrine, also call adrenalin, is secreted by the adrenal medulla. Norepinephrine … help(s) control alertness and wakefulness and it normally has an excitatory effect on its target organs in the sympathetic nervous system. Dopamine may have either an excitatory or inhibitory effect on the postsynaptic potentials … It has been associated with many functions that comprise goals and objectives in music therapy such as movement, attention, learning and addictions."

[13] Antes.

[14] *ibid.*

[15] https://academic.oup.com/atp/article-abstract123/2/118/1134246.

[16] Lagrand, p. 266.

[17] Lund, p. 45.

[18] John 14:16, 26; 15:26; 16:7.

[19] Jenkins, p. 30.

[20] Heath, Judy, No Time For Tears: Coping with Grief in a Busy World, second edition, Chicago Review Press, Inc., Chicago, IL, 2015, p. 192.

Chapter Seventeen: What You Should Know

[1] http://www.definitions.uslegal.com/d/death-cerrtificate.

[2] news.gallup.com; the AARP puts this figure at sixty percent.

[3] Yeh, Michele, Attorney at Law, Interview on August 26, 2019.

[4] *ibid.*

[5] *ibid.*

[6] *ibid.*

[7] *ibid.*

[8] Rasnick, John, Attorney at Law. Legal Voice/Estate Planning Akron, Ohio. Interview on July 23, 2019.

[9] *ibid.*

[10] *ibid.*

[11] McQuillen, Peter, Director of Stewardship Initiatives, Christ Community Chapel, Hudson, Ohio. Interview on June 11, 2019.

APPENDIX A

Protocol Questions

My name is _____ _____. I have agreed to be interviewed about my wife's death. I have been informed as to the purpose of this interview, that it will be used to gather information toward the compiling of help for those recently bereaved due to the death of their wives; and that my identity will remain anonymous.

1. What was the name of your wife?

2. How long had you been married?

3. How long has it been since your wife died?

4. When was that?

5. What was your wife's age and your age when your wife died?

6. What was determined to be the cause of your wife's passing?

7. Had you known that your wife was declining due to an illness or was her death sudden and unexpected? If it was due to a prolonged illness, how long was she ill?

8. If you anticipated this event, was there something that still surprised you?

9. What role did the community of faith have in extending sympathy and/or support?

10. How could people have helped you better? Did you want help in coping with your loss?

11. What have those in your circle of friends and family done to assist you since your wife died?

12. Did or does your wife's family have a role in helping you cope with your loss? How did you own (extended) family assist in your loss?

13. Were you in any sense relieved at the passing of your wife?

14. In the days following your wife's passing, did you have regrets about things that you did not do for or say to you wife?

15. Tell me about your most difficult moments, before and after your wife's death.

16. If you experienced anger, to whom was it directed (clergy, doctor, family, hospital, insurance, medical staff)?

17. How would you have wanted people to respond to you when they realized you were a (recent) widower?

18. What are you glad that people did following the passing of your wife?

19. What were / are your "triggers" for times of greater sorrow?

20. Tell me about holidays and other special events; how has your routine been changed?

21. At what times does loneliness seem not so difficult? What do you do when you are lonely; how to make the loneliness go away?

22. What, if anything, is the awkward about being a widower?

23. What do you wish people would (not) do?

24. What do you wish they would stop doing, if anything?

25. What was the greatest trial during the year immediately following your loss?

26. What was the greatest temptation during that period? Are they the same now?

27. What has been your greatest comfort in your bereavement?

28. Under what social conditions do you feel most comfortable? Most Awkward? What do you avoid altogether?

29. Did you seek individual help or group counseling? Why or why not?

30. If you had to describe a change in you brought about by this experience, what would you say that would be? If you have changed, how have you changed?

31. In one sentence, what advice would you give to the recent widower?

32. Much change has come into your life. In what ways has the passing of your wife changed you?

APPENDIX B

Possible Funeral Related Costs Considerations

- Preparation of the body
  Embalming
  Dressing: hair, nails, jewelry, makeup

- Use of staff, facilities and equipment
  Funeral ceremony at the funeral home
  Visitation at the funeral home
  Memorial service conducted at another facility

- Graveside service
- Transfer of remains to funeral home: Miles transported
- Automotive Equipment
  Casket coach
  Funeral sedan
  Service vehicle

- Miscellaneous merchandize
  Acknowledgment cards
  Visitor Registry

- Memorial cards
- Container for cremation
- Niche opening
- Casket
- Other burial container (urn)
- Forwarding remains to another funeral home
- Direct cremation
- Immediate burial
- Flowers
- Cemetery preparation

- Vault service fee
- Clergy
- Special music
- Obituary notices (Newspapers, etc.)
- Certified copies of Death Certificates
- Hairdresser, manicurist
- Cremation permit
- Burial permit
- Other optional items
- Taxes

APPENDIX C

Planning the Funeral

General Information

- What is the full legal name of the deceased?
- What is the date of birth?
- What is the date of death?
- What is the name of the spouse?
- What are the names of the living and deceased children?
- What are the names of the parents if living?
- What are the names of the siblings?
- Who should be notified of the death?

Service Information

- When is the funeral?
- Who will conduct the funeral service(s)?
- What music will be used; sung by, ? Played by ?
- What is the funeral director's name; his or her phone number?
- Will there be a separate graveside service?
- Will there be a separate memorial service?
- Will the casket, if used, be open or closed at the services?
- Will there be a private viewing for the family prior to or after the service?
- Will tributes be part of a service? If so, will they be written (suggested time 3-5 min.)
- What scripture(s) will be read?
- What poems or other readings be used?
- Who will offer prayers?
- Will there be a bulletin or a printed order of service? Who will prepare it?
- What time of day is the service?

Logistical Information

- Where is the funeral to take place?
- Will a map be provided for those attending the funeral from out of town?
- If there is cremation, will the urn be present at the funeral or memorial service?
- Who are the actual and/or honorary pallbearers; who will contact them to request that they serve?
- Will ushers be used; who will contact them to request that they serve?
- Will there be a picture board or digital media presentation? Who will arrange for these?
- Where is the burial to take place (cemetery or mausoleum name and location)?
- Will interment be out of state?
- Who will take care of a guest registry?
- Will the service(s) be recorded, videoed, or live-streamed?
- Will taking pictures be allowed?
- Will there be refreshments or a gathering/greeting after the funeral service?
- Where would a gather and greet take place? What is the expected attendance?

Auxiliary Information

- Is there a favorite charity or memorial fund to which contributions may be made?
- Will the family be notified of the donors?
- Will there be additional meal help for the family?
- Will there be a pre-service gathering of the family with the minister? Where will that take place?

INDEX

Dennis Disselkoen is available for book interviews and personal appearances. For more information contact:

Dennis Disselkoen
C/O Advantage Books
P.O. Box 160847
Altamonte Springs, FL 32716
info@advbooks.com

To purchase additional copies of these books, visit our bookstore at:
www.advbookstore.com

Longwood, Florida, USA
"we bring dreams to life" ™
www.advbookstore.com

CPSIA information can be obtained
at www.ICGtesting.com
Printed in the USA
LVHW081448270721
693840LV00020B/88